# Habitation of Dragons

Other books by Keith Miller

*The Taste of New Wine*
*A Second Touch*

# Keith Miller

·⁺⊰⊱⁺·

# Habitation
# of
# Dragons

*A book of hope about
living as a Christian.*

·⁺⊰⊱⁺·

Word Books, Publisher

Waco, Texas—London, England

*Library of Congress Catalog Card Number: 72–123009*

*Printed in the United States of America*

*To Mary Allen, Emma, Gene, and Floyd, each of whom gave invaluable help and encouragement . . . without which, in the end, the dragons might have written a book about me.*

# To the Reader

Some years ago I began to look for books which would describe the kind of *inner* Christian life which would lead one to an *outer* vulnerable involvement with other people.

Occasionally, I would find a writer who dared to admit an inner problem with which I wrestled regularly. And the release I experienced in finding a fellow struggler was tremendous. To know that I am not alone with the shameful dragons I fight in my inner life is very encouraging. Somehow the knowledge that others face these problems makes them not quite so fearsome in their habitation in my mind. Paradoxically, I discovered that the more of my own self-centeredness and sin I see and confess to God, the more free I feel to relate to other people who have problems in the world.

The Christian life is a very positive but often a painful experience for me. God seems to urge me forward to grow and learn. And I want to go on. But I resist the truth about myself because it is painful and threatening to see my imperfections and to try to change . . . even for Him. This book is not meant to be a substitute for your own prayers and thoughts but only some footprints of a Christian wanderer on the inner journey who is finding tremendous hope in the midst of life.

I have written these pages for men and women who would like to try to spend a few minutes every day thinking and praying about the problems of the Christian way. The book was not designed to be read straight through, but one "day" at a time—either by individuals or study groups who are hoping they will be led beyond themselves to love others. The format is very simple. Traditionally, the principal ways Christians have sought to determine God's will for their lives have been: (1) In the Scriptures, (2) through prayer, (3) in the lives and writings of other men, and (4) through personal experience. So for each of 42 days I have described a personal problem, related it to the thought of an outstanding writer, prayed about the situation as I have tried to face it, and indicated a passage of Scripture which seems relevant. The issues and dilemmas included are some of those of a writer and speaker who is also a business consultant. They do not represent the "ideal," "average," or the "most acceptable" problems a Christian should have. I realize that some of them may be foreign to your life. Many of the experiences were taken directly from my journal, kept during the past 20 years. Actual names and descriptions in the stories have been changed in most cases.

The pronoun "I" is on almost every page. For this I have no apology, since these experiences and problems are part of my own life. I am not posing as the world's worst sinner, nor as its most humble saint. But I have used this personal form in the hope that what is written may serve as a kind of mirror in which some of you may see some aspects of your own inner lives with Christ.

The idea of self-examination and commitment taking place in a wilderness setting came from Jesus' 40 days in the desert after His baptism (Matthew 4:1–11; Mark 1:12,13). Traditionally, many churches have used the 40 days before Easter each year as a time for self-examination and redirection. If you would like to use this book for that period, you can begin with the first "Wednesday" in the book, and you will finish the last reading Easter morning.

The title is from a passage in the 35th chapter of Isaiah (KJV) in which the author tells us that one day the Lord will make that frightening and desolate place which is the habitation of dragons into a green new land, and through this land He will build a highway . . . which shall be called the way of holiness.

Keith Miller
Austin, Texas

# Acknowledgments

Because of the spectrum of subjects covered here, several friends were good enough to read this manuscript in very rough form and give me specific suggestions concerning relevance and continuity. For this I am especially grateful to Brooks Goldsmith, Charles Sumners, Vester Hughes, Ann Hutchinson, Bruce Larson, Ralph Osborne, Leslie and Kristin Miller, and Gene Warr, who also helped me immeasurably in the selection of the Bible verses. Since I did not follow all their suggestions, I cannot blame these people for the shortcomings and mistakes you will find.

At one point, when the telephone and doorbell seemed about to swamp this project, our dear friends Loise and Joe Wessendorf called and suggested I go to their beautiful retreat center in central Texas to finish the writing. I did, and was deeply moved and refreshed by the time spent there.

Emma Ward patiently typed and retyped these pages and helped our editor, Floyd Thatcher, and my loving wife and best friend, Mary Allen, with detailed corrections and personal support.

I would also like to acknowledge the guiding Christian friendship of "Walter's bunch," the St. David's prayer therapy crew, and Bob Slocum, Richard Bauer and Douglas Harrell. Dick and Doug died during the time this manuscript was being written. Their clear-eyed facing of cancer and their own death not only affected this book but changed my life.

# Contents

# Contents

Habitation of Dragons

Then the eyes of the blind shall be opened,

and the ears of the deaf unstopped;

Then shall the lame man leap as a hart,

and the tongue of the dumb sing;

For in the wilderness shall the waters break out,

and streams in the desert.

And the parched ground shall become a pool,

and the thirsty land springs of water:

In the habitation of dragons, where each lay,

shall be grass with reeds and rushes.

And a highway shall be there, and a way,

and it shall be called The way of holiness . . .

Isaiah 35:5–8 (KJV)

# Nothing Wasted

THE FEAR of failure has played a fascinating backstage role in my life. In looking across the years I can see that I have made a good many of my decisions on the basis of this fear.

As a boy, I remember choosing sports in which I was reasonably sure I could do well and avoiding those in which I was likely to be beaten. And it was not only sports. I made a good many choices on the basis of *"not* failing." This was true even though I was quite willing to start at the bottom and make mistakes of all kinds while learning the fundamentals of those activities I did choose.

As I grew up, I came to see that this insecurity is related to a deeper and more profound doubt about my masculine adequacy, which makes me overcompensate continually to prove myself. But the outward effect has been that I have had great difficulty in making decisions which involve risking my reputation. Although I was not conscious of it, I was afraid of failing because I pictured the consequences as being devastating. I should have made a vocational change years before I did, but I was afraid to risk it. "What if I didn't make it on my own? What if I failed?" So I stayed where I was, miserable, but afraid to take a chance, expecting that a great specter "failure" would somehow cripple me for life if I did. No amount of pointing to past accomplishments or acknowledged ability seemed to put this fear to rest. So I stayed where I was.

When I became a Christian, I knew that this kind of anxious behavior was certainly not the freedom and abundant life of which Christ spoke. But I still had the pattern of inner indecision and fear about my own future when I thought about stepping out on my own. Outwardly, I was very decisive in other areas, which served to hide my inner inadequacy in this one. But in my mind I knew I was a real prisoner when it came to risking a radical vocational change.

Several years later, through a series of circumstances which almost forced me to decide, I changed jobs. Then, within a period of less than five years I made five changes of occupation—each time feeling as if the new change were definitely in line with God's will as I could see it. Somehow this feeling helped me to risk failure. I know that some of our friends must have thought I was off my rocker and headed for disaster. But I was working hard and finding out a great deal about the various worlds through which we moved during those years.

The important thing I learned is that for a Christian *nothing* is wasted in this life: no bad decision, no vocational change, no personal failure. I am deeply interested in the communication of the gospel of Jesus Christ to modern man. And my four years of Business Administration training, as well as the fifteen years I spent in the oil exploration business, are in some ways more helpful to me in communicating with laymen now than the four years I spent doing graduate work in theological schools. Every directional choice which seemed to be wrong along the way was to become a kind of "drawbridge" which would let me into a specific vocational

or social world later . . . worlds which would have been
closed to me if I had gone directly into "the ministry."

When I broke my back and thought that I was going to be
paralyzed from the neck down, when my parental family was
destroyed by sickness and accident, and when I did not get a
certain crucial promotion, such tragedies seemed so meaning-
less and wasteful. Yet these and other disappointments provided the only doorways I now have into the hearts and lives
of struggling men and women. For many of them live with
tragedy and disappointments and are also afraid to make
decisions which involve risk. Finally, it was my inability to be
able to control my circumstances which led me to begin to
turn my life toward God.

Now I have less trouble making decisions than ever before
in my life. I think this is partly because I know that even if I
fail (and I never *want* to fail), that I will see how God meets
a man in that particular kind of situation. The experience
at least may help me to understand those people I will meet
tomorrow or next year who will be going through the jungle
of failure and dying to their images of success. And I have
found a good bit of release from the fear of failure in this
discovery that nothing has to be wasted in a life with God.

··✦✧✦··

"Much as I long to be out of here, I don't believe a
single day has been wasted. What will come out of my
time here it is too early to say. But something is bound to
come out of it . . ."[1]

Dietrich Bonhoeffer
*Prisoner for God*

··✦✧✦··

Once when Mahatma Gandhi was twenty-four years
old he was working as an attorney in South Africa. He

boarded an overnight train with a first class ticket. At
Maritzburg a white man got on, looked at Gandhi, and
went to get two railroad officers. When they tried to get
him to leave the first class compartment, he showed them
his ticket and refused to move. Gandhi was thrown off
the train onto the station platform at the next stop. Years
later Dr. John R. Mott, an American missionary in
India, asked Mahatma Gandhi what had been the most
creative experiences in his life. And Gandhi told him
about the experience at Maritzburg. For here it was that
the mild little Indian's life was redirected to fight the
ugliness of color prejudice with the most unusual weap-
ons in history: love and non-violent resistance.[2]

Louis Fischer (paraphrased)
*Gandhi*

··+◀❖▶+··

DEAR GOD, help me in my weakness not to be afraid to live
and to try my wings in directions which seem right for me and
my family. On the other hand, keep me from using this
freedom to rationalize and run away from responsibility
when the present situation gets rough. Help me to realize
today that I am free either to stay or go, knowing that You
can take the failures and mistakes resulting from my bad
decisions and some day possibly turn them into wisdom and
sensitivity in relations with other people. Pray for me, Lord, I
do not know how to pray about success and failure. So often I
have been wrong in determining that which I thought would
be best for me.

··+◀❖▶+··

"Likewise the Spirit helps us in our weakness; for we
do not know how to pray as we ought, but the Spirit
himself intercedes for us with sighs too deep for words.
And he who searches the hearts of men knows what is the

mind of the Spirit, because the Spirit intercedes for the saints according to the will of God.

"We know that in everything God works for good with those who love him, who are called according to his purpose."

Romans 8:26–28

# The Incompleteness of
# "Total Honesty"
### (Problem of Integrity No. 1)

T WAS STILL very dark, but I was awake, having been disturbed by a bad dream. I was weeping because the dream
had recalled an experience in my adolescence which was so
painful that I thought I would never be free from its haunting
presence. Several times over the years I had been bothered by
this dream. And it always made me cringe, wanting to undo
something I had done as a teenager.

This experience and its painful reliving over the years had
changed my whole life, especially my views concerning integrity, love, and honesty in close relationships. And although I
hated the memory and had prayed many times that God
would erase it from my mind, there was no doubt that it had
helped me as a husband, father, and friend.

It had happened at a boys' summer camp where I was a
counselor after my freshman year in college. I was in charge
of a cabin full of junior boys, about eight and nine years old.
They were at the hero-worship age, and I really loved them.
One boy, Mortey, an orphan from somewhere in eastern Okla-
homa, was a particular favorite of mine. We became very

**20**

close friends. He was in my canoe on the float trip and played the starring comedy role in the play I wrote and ramrodded as tribe coordinator. He was a cagey little performer and stole the show with his quick grasp of humor. Although they teased Mortey about his weight and the fact that he wore glasses, he was outgoing and had lots of old-fashioned guts and intelligence.

The little guy used to reach up and take my hand when we were walking alone, as if I were his dad. And I would look down at him and smile. He tended to be a little cocky about everything, including his relationship with me—though he never acted that way when he thought I was around.

At the end of eight weeks the time came for the camp awards. The counselors met to vote on the honor camper trophies—the most important symbols of acceptance and success a boy could win. When the preliminary weeding out had been done, two boys remained in the race for junior honor camper: Mortey and Bobby. Wanting to have integrity, I decided I was so biased I could not vote, but when the ballots had been counted, both boys had the same number. I had to vote to break the tie.

At that time in my life I was an obsessive compulsive on the inside, and a joking character on the outside. But I had been taught that absolute integrity was the highest value; and, when decisions which seemed to concern my integrity were to be made, I really strained to do the right thing.

As I looked at these two boys and their camp records, I tried to be objective. Bobby was a much better athlete and had broken some records, but Mortey definitely had the edge in the human understanding department. They had both helped their tribes by winning contests and by being friendly kids. It was easy to see why the vote had been tied. I was miserable. Little Mortey had done a great job . . . but he *was* a little cocky, and he did have a few faults I knew about. This definitely gave Bobby a slight edge. Everyone knew how close we had been; and if I voted for Mortey, I was afraid the other counselors would think I was voting for him because of our friendship. It was strange that such a trivial thing could have been so momentous, but my whole integrity seemed to be on the line, and I felt sort of sick at my stomach. I did not want the responsibility of deciding.

My hesitation over the simple decision was delaying the meeting, and the other counselors became irritated. Under this pressure I decided—against Mortey. And we went on.

Only inside I didn't go on. I knew that although I had been honest, I had somehow been wrong. While sitting there, I got the idea that I ought to level with Mortey about what had happened. I tried to dismiss the thought, but it kept coming back. And I felt I *had* to tell him the truth "in order to have integrity" in the situation.

On the last morning at camp, as all the boys were getting on the bus, Mortey came up to me. Everyone was yelling for him to hurry. His face was streaked with tears, and it was obvious that he had been crying and did not want me to know. As we walked away from the others, I told him how much our friendship meant to me. I went on to tell him how close he had come to being elected honor camper—that in fact the vote had been a tie. His eyes got very wide, and I continued in my nineteen-year-old total honesty, "I hadn't voted up 'til that time, Mortey, because everyone knows that you and I are such close friends. But they made me vote then . . . and I voted for Bobby." As I started to explain why I had done it, the look on his face caught me completely off guard. I will never forget it. It haunts me still, because I saw the look of a soul betrayed by his dearest friend. In an instant I saw how wrong I had been and why. This little boy really loved me. And I realized that he *had* done a much finer job than Bobby at camp. But because Mortey had loved me, he had revealed his faults as well as his good points to me, and I had used this knowledge to judge and condemn him (from his perspective).

He just stood there and stared at me in disbelief. After his dad had let him down by leaving his mother, he had trusted me. I had the chance to give him all he had ever wanted, but I had tossed it to another boy in a different tribe, whom I hardly knew. He covered his face with his hands and ran toward the bus. I tried to grab him, to explain my feelings; but he broke loose and, wriggling between the last few campers, disappeared onto the bus. The door closed and the bus pulled out. I ran along beside it, hunting for Mortey in the windows. But all the other kids were pressed against them, and I didn't see him at all. In the midst of the shouting and singing of the camp loyalty song, Mortey rode out of my life in a cloud of dust.

It was years later, after I became a Christian and began to understand myself and my problems more clearly, that I began to see the trap "honesty" can be. It had become my highest value: "honesty at any cost." This meant that I *worshiped* honesty. In my struggle to decide who should be honor camper, I had been so intent on maintaining my own integrity that the broader values in the judging situation had escaped me. And in any case, I was blind to the consequences of trying to clear my own skirts with Mortey by telling him all—not realizing that a nine-year-old boy could not understand me. Yet maybe he *did* understand me and that was what broke his heart.

For this little boy saw the world through a different set of eyes than I did. It was to be almost ten years before I began to put myself into the hands of One who saw life in the same way that Mortey did. For in his world there was a higher

value than raw honesty with which to judge people . . . and
that value is love.

··+❧+··

"If he actually did it (was honest) for the sake of
having a good conscience, he would become a Pharisee
and cease to be a truly moral person. I think that even
saints did not care for anything other than simply to
serve God, and I doubt that they ever had it in mind to
become saints. If that were the case, they would have
become only perfectionists rather than saints."[3]

Viktor E. Frankl<br>
Man's Search for Meaning

··+❧+··

LORD, help me to realize the limited nature of my ability to
judge the total circumstances in any human encounter. Forgive me for being blinded by needs for integrity and putting
my adolescent desire for rightness ahead of Mortey's need
for love. But, God, thank You for teaching me through that
little boy the importance of the kind of loving loyalty You
have for us which transcends all your gifts including faith,
and even Your judgment of that which we deserve.

··+❧+··

"If I speak in the tongues of men and of angels, but
have not love, I am a noisy gong or a clanging cymbal.
And if I have prophetic powers, and understand all
mysteries and all knowledge, and if I have all faith, so
as to remove mountains, but have not love, I am nothing."

I Corinthians 13:1–2

# A Case for Purity

I AM CONTINUALLY amazed at some people who have been "born and raised" in the Christian faith, who tell me that I should talk about "victories" instead of problems. Last weekend I was conducting a conference for a group of deacons from a large church. It just happened that two of the witnesses I brought along had both been through a tough problem with adultery. This being a men's group, the witnesses in the opening session had talked about how rough it was to wrestle with the problems of extra-marital sex and how their despair had driven them to take a serious look toward God. But the discussion that followed was stilted and centered around church and organizational problems.

After the meeting that night the minister cornered me and was pretty upset. "I'm afraid you have the wrong group, Mr. Miller," he began. "These men I brought up here are converted Christians, deacons in my church. I know them all personally. If you keep dealing with these kinds of personal problems, I'm afraid you will lose our group's attention altogether."

I called our team together and told them we really had to pray, because the minister thought the participants were offended with us. After the team went to bed, I stayed in the office of the retreat center thinking of what we could do to recover our communication in the morning with a program which might meet the needs of thirty converted deacons. As I sat there alone late at night, there was a knock on the door. It was one of the deacons. After a long talk and prayer with this man, he left and went to bed, only to be followed by another, and then another. Five of the deacons came in that night to confess the same kinds of sex problems the witnesses had mentioned. They wanted to know if we honestly thought there was forgiveness and freedom for them—since they were committed Christians and yet had these same difficulties. I told them that I thought that there was forgiveness. And in each case after their confession we thanked God for His forgiveness and for a new chance.

The next day we faced a happy bunch of men. They were clustered around the two witnesses and were very warm and friendly. The men were open and seemed to care about each other. Their conversation now centered around how to reach other people in their town and help them to find freedom in Christ.

The minister was ecstatic to see his deacons befriending their "weaker brothers," the witnesses. When he pointed this out to me, I had to agree that here was indeed a group of deacons with an unusual degree of involvement.

The group got together before leaving. And when the minister found out what had actually happened, he said he was shocked at first, then thoughtful, and then in some way relieved that they did not have to pretend to each other any more that there are no serious problems for the committed Christian man to confess. And he thanked the two lay witnesses who thought they had failed.

*·+❋+·*

"For him who confesses, shams are over and realities have begun; he has exteriorized his rottenness. If he has not actually got rid of it, he at least no longer smears it over with a hypocritical show of virtue—he lives at least upon a basis of veracity . . . The complete decay of the practice of confession in Anglo-Saxon communities is a little hard to account for . . . One would think that in more men the shell of secrecy would have had to open, the pent-in abscess to burst and gain relief, even though the ears that heard the confession were unworthy."[4]

William James
*The Varieties of Religious
Experience*

Private confession to a brother . . . "is useful, even necessary, and I would not have it abolished. Indeed, I rejoice that it exists in the church of Christ, for it is a cure without equal for distressed consciences. For when we have laid bare our conscience to our brother and privately made known to him the evil that lurked within, we receive from our brother's lips the word of comfort spoken by God himself. And, if we accept this in faith, we find peace in the mercy of God speaking to us through our brother."[5]

Martin Luther
*Works*, Vol. 36

*·+❋+·*

LORD, I don't know who started the notion that being a Christian, or a deacon, or even a bishop somehow seals one's life off from the problems of the world. But I wish You would tell whoever it was to stop saying it. Teach us to accept Your forgiveness and the power to change our lives. But when we trip and fall, help us to confess our sins, get up, and go on loving and helping people in Your name. Keep us from being naïve whitened sepulchers who cannot accept the stark fact of failure in our lives . . . and therefore Your forgiveness available to us through Jesus Christ.

⋯⊷⊱⊰⊶⋯

"If we say we have no sin, we deceive ourselves, and the truth is not in us. If we confess our sins, he is faithful and just, and will forgive our sins and cleanse us from all unrighteousness."

I John 1:8,9

# "You Don't Listen to Me Any More!"

Y OU DON'T listen to me any more!" I blurted out, right in the middle of a sentence I was "delivering."

"Why, I *do too*," Mary Allen answered in what seemed like genuine surprise.

But I did not believe her. After a week of traveling on a speaking trip, I am usually a highly tuned listener to individuals with whom I have been counseling. And I can usually spot it when someone is not paying attention to what *I* am saying. When I first started traveling, Mary Allen pumped me for details about each trip as soon as I got home. Often I did not feel like "replaying" the meeting, but she wanted to hear, so I would. But now something had happened. She still asked about the trips, but then seemed to get diverted by almost any kind of interruption, often just as I was getting into something which was very exciting to me. This really bugged me, and I would get furious. If she didn't want to listen, then why did she ask? . . . and then not pay attention. Maybe she was getting bored with me. After all, we had been married seventeen years.

Anyway, I was furious when this happened yesterday. I

had just come home from a seven-day trip. The two meetings I had attended were made up of very sharp couples. Although many of the people did not agree with some of the things I was saying and doing, they gave me the great compliment of listening to me. In counseling sessions and social visits between the larger meetings, people who came to see me could not have been more attentive, and I was conscious of being very open and receptive to each of them.

But when I got home, here was this seeming indifference. Being a neurotic, I conjured up reasons for Mary Allen's behavior, all of which boiled down to the facts that (1) she was not interested in that which I was doing and (2) she was not interested in me. And after a couple of hours of unexplained resentment and cutting remarks—which had the desired effects of making us both miserable—I let my problem out in the open.

Following the initial expression of feelings back and forth, we began to talk about what had happened. Being so mad at her, I had a hard time hearing what she was saying. But one thing echoed in my mind as I drove toward the office later: "When you come home from these speaking trips you act like a spoiled king!"

That hurt! And particularly because I had the sneaking suspicion that it just might be true—although it had not occurred to me before that my behavior and attitudes had changed upon returning from trips during the past couple of years, at least not in a *negative* way.

As I thought about this, I wondered how many lay speakers, ministers, doctors, bank presidents—people who get lots of personal attention and affirmation in their vocational lives —I wondered how many such men begin unconsciously to behave like spoiled kings without even knowing that it is happening. I wondered how many other men begin unconsciously to expect their wives and families to hang on their words and attend to their needs with the same speed and solicitousness their hosts at meetings or their secretaries do? I started not to write this because it is difficult for me to accept this about myself. Since I consciously want it not to be true, I would like to deny it to myself, and especially to you. But I am afraid it is true.

I realized that one of the things which makes it so bad— and I think may even exaggerate it in the eyes of a wife—is the fact that important unshared experiences often separate people. That is, when I have been off to a stimulating seminar alone, I often make the mistake of coming home and very excitedly telling Mary Allen about a "fantastic place," or person, or group, which has changed my life. In one sense she is glad. But in another sense, the experience which she did not share separates us, because I am implying that I am "going on" due to what happened to me. And since she was not pres-ent, there is an implication that I am leaving her behind—or perhaps an unconscious fear on her part that I might—even though that is not what I am saying or thinking.*

All this does not mean that I am suddenly going to quit talking about trips and conferences when I come home. That would really cause problems. But I am going to attempt to be more thoughtful concerning the *way* I talk about them. I hope I will not forget to find out first what has been going on at home to laugh or cry about while I have been away. And I am going to try not to expect a woman with two teenage daughters —and a third on the teenage threshold—to suddenly stop the world in which she has been operating alone for a week, to cheer at my recital of the great time I have had (away from home responsibilities) as an "honored guest" somewhere.

---

* Of course this situation can be reversed in cases where the wife is the conference-going religious fanatic of the family.

"But I am sure my readers understand the subtle temptation which assails me: that of trying to be the personage I am expected to be. It slips in disguised as an honest concern for the proper fulfilment of my vocation. . . .

"In order not to disappoint them I ought to tell them only of my positive experiences. In fact they are always disconcerted at first when I speak of my own difficulties, doubts and failings. But they soon come to see that this atmosphere of truth brings us closer and binds us together. My experience of the power of God means more to them than it would if they thought me a quite different sort of person from themselves."[6]

Paul Tournier
*The Meaning of Persons*

LORD, forgive me for my self-centered blindness to my own insensitivity. Give me the insight to see the effect of my real behavior on other people and on You. And then, Lord, please give me the courage and strength to confess my sin and change my actions. Thank You, God, that You are in the life-changing business.

"For by the grace given to me I bid every one among you not to think of himself more highly than he ought to think, but to think with sober judgment, each according to the measure of faith which God has assigned him."

Romans 12:3

# Do It Unto Me

AFTER TEN years of making the attempt to commit my life to God, most of my close personal relationships had been deeply affected. I still could not keep them all straightened out, but had found an open style of relating that made confession, forgiveness, beginning again—and sometimes change—possible with my family and close associates.

But as I watched the news and talked to college students and black groups, the question began to plague me: "How does this openness lead Christians out into the world to become vulnerably involved with Christ in the *social* agony around us?" I couldn't find any rules for this. But some of us began getting involved with people who had real material needs as a result of a small group which meets at 6:30 on Monday mornings.

We had started this group to begin to learn in a safe, loving atmosphere how to communicate about the hope and meaning we were finding inside our lives, where we had been so alone with our faith. This was not an "honesty cult" in which to confess our lurid sins, nor was it a pietistic clique; but it was a place to begin facing openly the troubles and problems we had in living, working, and praying, which kept us from being God's people and doing His will.

As the months went by, we tried to help each other to
investigate and discover the shape our lives and ministries
might take in our own community. That was when I began to
become acutely conscious of some of the social problems we
have. And as we started to share this inward journey with
Christ and with each other, some of us were led beyond our
own horizons and out into the world in ways we never could
have anticipated.

One of the men in this group was named George. He is a
successful and wealthy home builder and real estate devel-
oper. But George had spent part of his youth in an orphan's
home and knew what it was like to have very little. He had
made a commitment of his life to Christ a few years earlier
and had begun to relearn to live. One morning George came
into the group and was very thoughtful. "I woke up at four
o'clock this morning," he said, "and I couldn't go back to
sleep. I was praying and discovered an amazing thing—I love
niggers!" George had tears in his eyes. Having been raised as
a southern boy, he didn't see anything incongruous about
what he had said. He went on, "But if I love them, I guess
God would want me to do something to help them wouldn't
He?" We supposed so. "I would like for you to pray that I'll
be able to find out what I can do to help Christ with the race
situation *here in town.*" And we did pray that, although I felt
a restlessness in my own life as we prayed.

The next week George came to the meeting excited, but
uncertain. "They've asked me to serve on the human relations
commission, and they want me to come out with a public
statement in favor of open housing. I went around to the other
realtors in town and they said, 'We think that would be a
great thing for *you* to do, George,' but none of them would go
along on the statement. So I checked a national realtor's study
and found out that, in the price range of my homes, if a black

family moves in, the surrounding property values decline at once and quite a bit." He stopped a minute. "What I found out was that this public stand on open housing might ruin me financially." We wrestled with George in his dilemma that morning and finally told him that whatever he decided, we hoped that he would not make the statement because of guilt, but only if he thought it was God's will for him.

The following week the whole business came to a head. George said he had been looking into the problem and praying about what to do when he remembered something Elton Trueblood had told our group a few weeks before. It was the old story about the man who had the crazy notion that he wanted to walk across Niagara Falls on a tightrope pushing a wheelbarrow with a man in it. He set up two poles in his backyard, stretched a tightrope between them, and practiced every day for a year—first with a balance bar, then without it, then with a wheelbarrow, and finally he added a load of 175 pounds of bricks. And he never fell off the wire. His next-door neighbor watched every evening, and the crowds got larger each day as the time drew near. The press picked up the story, and when the big moment came, a huge throng was on hand. The fellow with the wheelbarrow appeared to be a little nervous as he stood looking out across the wire. He turned to his faithful neighbor and asked, "Joe, do you believe I can do it?"

Slapping him confidently on the back Joe said, "I absolutely believe you can. I bet a tenth of this year's income on you."

The performer looked out over the falls and then asked once more, "Joe, do you *really* believe?"

Joe said seriously, "I *really believe.*"

"Fine," the other fellow replied, "*you're* my man. Get in the wheelbarrow."

Then George said quietly to the rest of us in the group,
"This week the Lord said to me 'George, if you trust Me with
your future, get in the wheelbarrow on this race thing.' And I
did."

This is not a story with a happy ending. It cost George
about a hundred thousand dollars the first year and some
painful rejection in our city. We don't know yet how much
more it will cost him. But something happened to several of
us in that group about that same time. Two ministers granted
use of their church educational wing for a head start program
downtown during the week. And there is now a free medical
clinic in that church being run by an interdenominational
group for poor people who can't qualify for other help. I
started to try to talk to black groups and learn about the real
issues in the racial struggles. And several of us began to be
haunted about ways we might help Christ with the poor people in our city.

This beginning to move out, beyond my own personal and
business associations, took place for me because a man let a
few of us share in his struggle against a life-long prejudice,
and we watched him—afraid, wonderful—as he climbed in
the wheelbarrow for Jesus Christ . . . and for some black
men and women and little children—who will never know.

I do not know how much we can do, and sometimes I am
afraid of the hostility of people whose backgrounds and circumstances are different from my own. Sometimes the race
and poverty situations seem so hopeless that I just want to run
away and forget them. But I pray that I will not. Because as I
get closer to people who appear to be different from me, I find
that most of the real differences are in my mind. And as I
take small, specific steps to go and do things which need
doing, I realize that Christ is probably not as concerned with

measuring the magnitude of my effectiveness . . . as with whether or not I go.

·•+◆❖◆+•·

"Faith without ethical consequences is a lie. Good works must necessarily follow faith. God does not need our sacrifices but he has, nevertheless, appointed a representative to receive them, namely our neighbor. The neighbor always represents the invisible Christ."[7]

J. S. Whale
*Christian Doctrine*

·•+◆❖◆+•·

LORD, thank You that You have not called upon me to be all-powerful or omnipresent but only to be a part of a larger family, a team. Forgive me when I try to pitch, catch, hit, and manage the entire team all at the same time. But help me to have enough sense and courage to play the position You have given me in this changing world, even if it's not in the "big leagues." Somehow in my megalomania it is hard for me to participate when I cannot lead or when I cannot at least see the hope of solving the whole problem through my efforts. Help me to learn the value to You of a "cup of cold water" where it's really needed and how to use a bucket to wash some tired smelly feet—without an audience.

·•+◆❖◆+•·

"Then the King will say to those at his right hand, 'Come, O blessed of my Father, inherit the kingdom prepared for you from the foundation of the world; for I was hungry and you gave me food, I was thirsty and you gave me drink, I was a stranger and you welcomed me, I was naked and you clothed me, I was sick and you visited me, I was in prison and you came to me.' Then the righteous will answer him, 'Lord, when did we see thee hungry and feed thee, or thirsty and give thee

drink? And when did we see thee a stranger and welcome thee, or naked and clothe thee? And when did we
see thee sick or in prison and visit thee?' And the King
will answer them, 'Truly, I say to you, as you did it to
one of the least of these my brethern, you did it to me.' "

Jesus Christ
Matthew 25:34–40

# Change of Life

LAST NIGHT I visited with a friend. He is younger than I, but he looks like a tired old man, and he is very sick physically. I can still see his haunted eyes. The urgency he now feels about his health made me starkly aware of the reality of my own aging. As I thought about life and its changes, I realized what a strange little creature I am. One minute I am a big virile male with the world by the tail. But I can be deflated in an instant by the first sign of diminishing sexual virility or genuine rejection. I get depressed and insecure sometimes and find myself imagining and doing all kinds of irrational things to bolster my fading youth.

I think it is unfortunate that we are not taught somewhere in our growing up that we men also go through a transition period psychologically comparable to "change of life" in women.* Life seems to be slipping by and it is not quite what we thought it would be. There is no longer that limitless sea of time ahead of us in this pilgrimage in which we find fulfillment. A kind of fear sets in.

I have never seen it this clearly before. All we usually feel

---

\* "It is now well established that men as well as women go through an involutional period." Kisker, George W., *The Disorganized Personality* (New York: McGraw-Hill, 1964), p. 377.

is that our wives are getting demanding or bossy or unreasonable. And there are more things that make us nervous, restless, and fearful than there used to be. But it is kind of comforting to know that all of this is just a part of the process of
living. I don't know what I would do if I had come to this
point in my life without God and fellow strugglers like you
with whom I can hope to find acceptance. Of course, sometimes when I look at the problems of old age and death, I
wonder if Christianity is a cruel joke and we are deluding
ourselves and missing our only chance to live it up. And a
panicky feeling stirs in my chest.

But at such times, my mind scans all the world's bright
opportunities and material signs of fulfillment for an option
to this life of faith, and I ask myself, "Of all the things you
have tried and tasted, what is more real than this relationship
with the living God and His people?" And whatever else that
has seemed important fades away. So I smile and sigh; and
again with a deep sense of release, I offer my life to Jesus
Christ and to the finding of His place for me in His family.
This is not done in desperation. But after years of trying to
find something to hang my life on, I have discovered that the
greatest achievements and philosophies about which I have
known are poor seconds to the clear hope and the sense of
ultimate acceptance and caring I have found in this experi-
mental life in Christ. And I am grateful that although the
problems and distresses of living may lay me low, they cannot
separate me from the love of God. In such moments I realize
that I have discovered a good direction for my life. And I get
up and go to work a happier person . . . as I am going to do
right now! Have a good day!

--+❊+--

"Proper recognition and appreciation of normal instincts leads the young person into life and entangles

him with fate, thus involving him in life's necessities and the consequent sacrifices and efforts through which his character is developed and his experience matured. For the mature person, however, the continued expansion of life is obviously not the right principle, because the descent towards life's afternoon demands simplification, limitation, and intensification—in other words, individual culture. A man in the first half of life with its biological orientation can usually, thanks to the youthfulness of his whole organism, afford to expand his life and make something of value out of it. But the man in the second half of life is oriented towards culture, the diminishing powers of his organism allowing him to subordinate his instincts to cultural goals. Not a few are wrecked during the transition from the biological to the cultural sphere. Our collective education makes practically no provision for this transitional period. Concerned solely with the education of the young, we disregard the education of the adult, of whom it is always assumed—on what grounds who can say?—that he needs no more education. There is an almost total lack of guidance for this extraordinarily important transition from the biological to the cultural attitude, for the transition of energy from the biological form into the cultural form."[8]

Carl Jung
*The Collected Works*, Vol. 8

Faith . . . "is a great art and doctrine, which no saint has learned and fathomed fully unless he has found himself in despair, in the anguish of death, or in extreme peril."[9]

Martin Luther
*Works*, Vol. XXIII

DEAR LORD, thank You for the signposts of physical change and death which force me to see the frail and transient nature of my life without You. I pray that in times of health and success I will not forget You and turn away. Give me the courage to face the stark realities of life and help me to move through each stage of development with a perspective of wisdom and joy instead of fear, knowing that You will be with me.

·••❦❧•··

"Who shall separate us from the love of Christ? Shall tribulation, or distress, or persecution, or famine, or nakedness, or peril, or sword? As it is written, 'For thy sake we are being killed all the day long; we are regarded as sheep to be slaughtered.' No, in all these things we are more than conquerors through him who loved us. For I am sure that neither death, nor life, nor angels, nor principalities, nor things present, nor things to come, nor powers, nor height, nor depth, nor anything else in all creation, will be able to separate us from the love of God in Christ Jesus our Lord."

Romans 8:35–39

# The Critical Eye

H E WAS an excellent speaker," I heard myself saying sincerely, "but I thought he had a real need to let us know how much he had read, and I wondered if this got in people's way as they listened to him."

I was talking to Mary Allen on the way home from hearing a brilliant and winsome Christian speaker at a meeting. We both responded to him as a person, but I had felt uneasy during his lecture.

This morning when I was going through my prayers and came to "confession," I found myself saying, "God, forgive me for tearing down our friend last night. He is a fine Christian communicator and I am very grateful that he can do things I cannot."

As I said these words of confession, I saw why I needed to confess. I have a habit of subtly undermining people who are better than I am at doing the things I do. At a conscious level I am deeply grateful for anyone who is an effective Christian communicator. But if he is speaking to the same group I am trying to reach and if he has a different style from mine, I must be threatened somehow—as if people may think the other man's way is right and mine is wrong. This has not been a conscious reaction, but in looking back across the years I can see that it has been true.

Now, when I catch myself subtly criticizing a talented Christian communicator, I hope I will be able to see the reason my sharp little eyes have detected a chink in his armor so that I can *truly* be thankful that he is a spokesman for our common Lord.

·+◆◆►+·

"Thou wilt never be an inwardly religious and devout man unless thou pass over in silence the shortcomings of thy fellow men, and diligently examine thine own weaknesses."[10]

Thomas à Kempis
*The Imitation of Christ*

". . . no one can get rid of the spirit of judgment by an effort of the will. As long as I am obsessed by a friend's fault which has shocked me and made me reproach him, no matter how much I say to myself; 'I do not wish to judge him,' I judge him none the less. But the spirit of judgment evaporates as soon as I become conscious of my own faults and speak freely of them to my friend, as he speaks to me of those which make him reproach himself.

". . . A man's judgment of another depends more on the one judging and on his passions than on the one being judged and his conduct."[11]

Paul Tournier
*Guilt and Grace*

·+◆◆►+·

GOD, sometimes I can't imagine how You can put up with me. I tell You one minute that I love You with all my heart, and *mean* it. But the next hour I am murdering a fellow Christian by undermining what he has done, by subtly criticizing him and calling attention away from his message about You to his weaknesses, which I seem to be an expert at locating. Forgive me, and give me a new start right now. Help me to keep observing and learning by other men's mistakes as well as my own. But give me the security to affirm them for the helpful things they say about You, rather than subtly attacking their personalities and thus indirectly Your attempts to love men through them.

·∙+⊹⧉⊹+∙·

"Why do you pass judgment on your brother? Or you, why do you despise your brother? For we shall all stand before the judgment seat of God; for it is written, 'As I live, says the Lord, every knee shall bow to me, and every tongue shall give praise to God.' . . . Then let us no more pass judgment on one another, but rather decide never to put a stumbling block or hindrance in the way of a brother."

Romans 14:10–13

# True Grit?

THIS MORNING I woke up from a dream with a scene still vivid in my imagination. I was reliving a terrifying day in my childhood—a day which changed my life. There I was, standing in line in the first grade room trying to appear cool and unperturbed. But when the first little boy screamed and struggled to get away from the doctor who was giving the shots, my heart pounded so loudly I was afraid everyone could hear it. I even hummed softly to be sure they did not. Struggling against a terrifying urge to run out the door, I tried to appear casual by looking out the window at the white billowing clouds in the Spring sky. Other kids were making sniffling noises as if they were about to tune up and cry also. I was hoping they would, so maybe the teacher would call this whole thing off.

When I glanced toward the front of the room to see what was happening, my mother, who was a volunteer helper, spoke quietly to the doctor and then came back in the line to where I was standing. She bent over and whispered in my ear, "We want you to come up and take your shot now to show the other boys and girls how to be brave. It really doesn't hurt much."

I was terrified but also very pleased to be the one chosen as

**46**

an example of courage. So I walked up to the doctor, calmly rolled up my sleeve, and stuck out my arm (as if I were only shaking hands—instead of about to get the needle).

I smiled as I remembered how proud my mother had been of me. She told my dad and older brother at dinner that night about my performance, and she mentioned my "courage" to a friend over the telephone. Somehow the die was cast. I *had* to be strong and courageous.

The only trouble was: I was not. I was afraid . . . of lots of things. But I acted courageously because I was more afraid of being found out than of the outward "dangers" and threats of life. So a pattern was established—one which caused me to be very anxious about possible exposure and made me feel inadequate inside, regardless of how well I performed in the arena of real life. I remember the paradoxical feelings once of being elected president of my high school class, making the ball team, and feeling very inadequate—all at the same time.

Then, the day came when I really understood that I am acceptable to God because of *His* loving and forgiving nature and not because of *my* ability or courage. I was overwhelmed. It was too good to be true. When I started to try to find His will as it impinged on my abilities and circumstances, I began to be free to admit my hidden fears and inadequacies to others who were afraid. Gradually, I started to reveal my inner self to God and to people, and some of them revealed themselves to me. I discovered some strange things about courage and inadequacy. Having always thought of those towering men who had a calm exterior in the face of danger as being unafraid, I was certain that some of them would think I was a chicken-hearted phony if they knew how I felt.

But the truth seems to be that many of them are scared, too, and have learned to hide their fears even from themselves. In fact I have discovered that the strongest people I know, the ones I would really want beside me in any real trouble or danger, are those who know that they are afraid, can admit it, and yet are willing to take risks for God and other people.

I don't know how or when it happened, but I am not nearly as afraid of people now as I once was. Possibly, this is because my greatest fear was not of real problems and threats, but of being found inadequate and rejected. Now I can sometimes risk revealing to others what seems to be more truly my real self. When they see "the frightened little boy" that I sometimes am inside and do not run away or laugh at me, I can more nearly believe their acceptance and affirmation when they offer it. Before I could not.

It seems to me that it is often very helpful to others to be strong and *not* reveal one's fear in the face of danger. But when the danger is over or when someone asks, it is strengthening to know that others were afraid too.

Somehow I think this paradox is near the heart of the kind of life presented in the gospel. God seems to be offering to use weak men and women who feel inadequate and incomplete to demonstrate in their courage a vulnerable kind of love and understanding the world seldom sees in the "strong and mighty ones."

&middot;&middot;+ +&middot;&middot;

"The adventurous life is not one exempt from fear, but on the contrary one that is lived in full knowledge of fears of all kinds, one in which we go forward in spite of our fears. Many people have the utopian idea that others are less afraid than they are, and they feel therefore that they are inferior. All men are afraid, even desperately afraid. If they think they are exempt from fear, that is because they have repressed their fears. Fear is part of human nature."[12]

Paul Tournier
*The Adventure of Living*

·+ ◄◈►·+·

LORD, thank You that in a paradoxical way the power revealed through human personality is seen to be more clearly Yours when it inhabits an otherwise weak person. Help me today to learn to depend more on Your strength and acceptance for the source of my courage instead of the flimsy shield of my confident mask.

·+ ◄◈►·+·

". . . 'My grace is all you need; power comes to its full strength in weakness.' I shall therefore prefer to find my joy and pride in the very things that are my weakness; and then the power of Christ will come and rest upon me. Hence I am well content, for Christ's sake, with weakness, contempt, persecution, hardship, and frustration; for when I am weak, then I am strong."

Jesus Christ and the Apostle Paul
II Corinthians 12:9, 10 (NEB)

# An Offensive Way to Hide

YESTERDAY I was miserable. I was cross and unreasonable with my family, and yet I desperately needed their love and acceptance. This usually means that I feel insecure about myself in some area—my work, my future, the children's happiness. But instead of facing my fears and anxieties, I become a gruff independent critic of the scene around me . . . at those points at which it touches my self-imposed solitude. My responses are cynical. And I point out the selfish or thoughtless aspects of everyone else's behavior in order to correct them, for their own good, of course. In short, I am obnoxious.

But inside, behind the barrage of rejection I am pouring out over my family, is a miserable person who does not understand why he is so intent on fouling his own nest. At such times I desperately want to be loved—in spite of the fact that I know that I do not deserve it.

It happened again yesterday. And last night I could not stop it. But before I went to sleep I was able to tell Mary Allen that I was sorry I was being so mean and that I did not consciously want to be. After telling her, I realized what the cause was. Yesterday morning, after meeting with you, I had a personal crisis about my own future and let Mary Allen see

the fear and immaturity I still have about my performance—
a fear with which I have been stuck since childhood. Since I
thought that specter had been buried and had said so, I was
disappointed in myself and had felt very vulnerable when
Mary Allen had seen my weakness. Then I guess I must have
unconsciously wanted to hurt her because I was so frustrated
at not being able to change my own feelings. At least I wanted
to get the spotlight off that particular fault of mine. This was
true in spite of the fact that she had been very understanding
and loving, and I had appreciated it. But I guess way down
inside I could not believe she loved me in my weakness—
after all, I couldn't even love myself.

And I saw that *this* was the deeper issue. When I am
unacceptable to myself, I often try to raise a furor of negative
reactions and signals, evidently hoping that in the confusion
no one will notice my weakness. You might call it the
"skunk" system. As everyone knows, when a skunk gets in
trouble, he puts out a cloud of horrible odor that the other
animals all know will stick to them if it gets on them. So
everyone else scrambles for cover, and when the "smoke"
clears, the skunk has walked to safety.

Don't feel superior if you do not handle your vulnerability
in this way. One of our little girls likes the "turtle" method,
which is simply to pull in her head and withdraw. After
everyone tries to sniff around and bring her out, we all walk
away, and she has arrived at a safe "place" in which she can
mope or feel sorry for herself in peace. Having checked with
several people, it seems that this method is more popular than
that of the skunk. But unfortunately I find it very difficult to
make a turtle shell out of a skunk skin.*

·+·+≡⊠+·+·

---

* It is astounding how many times skunks and turtles marry.

"How often we hide behind masks and hug delusions with compulsive passion because we are afraid to be known, to be loved—but in the nearness of real, deep, substantial love we run back to our masks of isolation, shallowness, and safety in terror of being revealed and accepted. We hide ourselves in acts of passion; we bury love under false prudence; we substitute biological pleasures for the divine wonder and peril of love; we surround ourselves with cold, icy barriers to defend the smug self from being shattered by love.

"It is easier to snub another ('snuff the light of his life out of our life') than to love. And so we indulge in spiritual assassination in order to protect our own convenience."[13]

William McNamara
*The Art of Being Human*

LORD, help me to keep short accounts with You by confessing my sins and fears as soon as I am aware of them. I don't want to hurt everyone around me in order to cover up my own needs and insecurities. Thank You that although I am more aware of my faults and incompleteness than I ever have been, I feel a strange buoyancy and strength in being able to live with the problems out in the world in my relationships. I don't understand why I am so ready to point out the faults of others as a defense to hide my own, but I would certainly appreciate some help as I begin to concentrate on not doing it.

"Judge not, that you be not judged. For with the judgment you pronounce you will be judged, and the measure you give will be the measure you get. Why do you see the speck that is in your brother's eye, but do not notice the log that is in your own eye? Or how can you say to your brother, 'Let me take the speck out of your

eye,' when there is a log in your own eye? You hypo-
crite, first take the log out of your own eye, and then you
will see clearly to take the speck out of your brother's
eye."

Matthew 7:1–5.

# The Difficult Is *Good?*

THIS MORNING I woke up feeling very uneasy with a strong urge to "escape." Suddenly I sat up in bed wondering, "What's the matter with you?" I thought about our lives and my job and realized that things are going well. We are all healthy and have enough to eat. Mary Allen and the children do not have any major problems. I am in the midst of writing this book. But I have the feeling that it is dull and you will not read it—or if you do, you will think I am naïve. So I will have to go through the agony of reworking the manuscript again to try to reproduce in writing the pictures which I see in my mind. And this is very difficult for me.

At this point I saw my problem. For some reason I was trying to avoid writing, the very thing I love to do. Why? As I thought back over my life, I realized that I have often avoided things I really wanted to do, just because they were difficult. I remember as a skinny little boy wanting to have a well proportioned physique. But I would do almost anything, including feigning sickness on occasion, to avoid heavy muscle-building work around our yard. I love to learn, and yet in school I avoided studying as long as possible.

Later, as an adult, I strongly resisted the notion of committing my life to God. Although I was strongly attracted to the idea and suspected that it was the better way, the suggestion of "total commitment" made me angry and was repelling. Such a commitment would no doubt fill my life with diffi- culties and force me to examine my true motivations at every turn. I was convinced that I would have to give up the normal joys and goals of life.

Throughout my life a strong desire has often forced me to overcome my resistance and try the more difficult thing: to begin doing the calisthenics, work, study in school, and fin- ally, to become a Christian. In each case, when I chose what appeared to be the difficult course, I learned a strange truth about life: The *difficulties* were actually the doorways to growth and fulfillment. Yet I have spent my life, both before and after becoming a Christian, unconsciously avoiding pain- ful and uncomfortable situations.

Yet, I realized this morning that most of the insights which have been of value to me in relating to other people were distilled from my own difficulties and pain in trying to wrestle with the problems of life. Some of these things—the conflict with loved ones, the blundering mistakes in trying to learn to pray at home—some of these seemed funny when I wrote or told about them in retrospect. But at the time I was *facing* the situations they were difficult, agonizing encounters from which I wanted to run—and often did.

I cannot recall a single person who has been of real help to me in learning to cope with life who has not personally faced some great difficulties or suffering in his own experience, even though he may have seemed profoundly positive and joyful.

The second thought which struck me was that the experi- ence we call "joy" does not usually come from the trouble- free and effortless periods of life. Rather, joy seems to be distilled from a strange mixture of challenge, risk, and hope. And as I have met in groups with other uncertain Christians to share the difficulties in our families, vocations, and relations with other people, the effect has often been one of deep joy and insight into life—even though the difficulties themselves may not have been overcome.

But if this is true, then I should not run from the risk of difficulty and responsibility as I have done so often. I should quit trying to avoid the challenge of hard tasks but instead thank God for them. Because these things seem to provide the main doorways to character and firsthand knowledge about life.*

My restlessness this morning must have been because I did not want to face the difficulty of writing these pages to you. But doing it has brought a great sense of peace about today. And I hope that for the rest of the day I will spend less time running from the tasks and problems that may lead me to life and wholeness.

··◆◆❖◆··

"People then should rejoice in suffering, strange as it sounds, for this is a sign of the availability of energy to transform their characters. Suffering is nature's way of indicating a mistaken attitude or way of behavior, and . . . to the non-egocentric person every moment of suffering is the opportunity for growth."[14]

Rollo May
*The Art of Counseling*

"Where there is no strife there is decay: 'The mixture which is not shaken decomposes.' "[15]

Heraclitus

---

* I am not saying that one should go out *looking* for personal pain and difficulties. This tendency can be a mental sickness called masochism. It has been my experience however that one will find plenty of problems and pain to face just trying to do God's will in his own life.

FATHER, thank You that Your Holy Spirit seems to use the hours of conflict and suffering which I experience as "teachable moments" in my life. Help me to distill from difficulties a way of living which is whole and gutty and does not sugarcoat reality. Give me the grace not to reject those Christians whose circumstances have been such that they have never personally faced the fear of failure and the frustration of suffering through something difficult. Thank You that Your presence with me in my weakness often brings endurance and hope.

"More than that, we rejoice in our sufferings, knowing that suffering produces endurance, and endurance produces character, and character produces hope, and hope does not disappoint us, because God's love has been poured into our hearts through the Holy Spirit which has been given to us."

Romans 5:3–5.

# Commitment: The End of the Trail Intellectually?

FOR A LONG time the notion of making a "total commitment to Christ" seemed like a kind of intellectual suicide to me. In some vague way I had gotten the idea that such a commitment would lead to a narrow, fragmented intellectual life made up of "religious" thoughts, books, and conversations on one hand, and "non-religious" ones on the other. I guess my sense of loyalty made me feel that once I "joined" Christ, I could never again question His existence or His way of life. Since I felt that I would be obligated to think "Christian thoughts," I believed that my mind could not roam in new fields and seek new truths with the freedom to examine anything—a freedom which is very important to me.

However, in the act of offering as much of my life as I could at a particular time to as much of Christ as I could grasp at that moment, I began to learn some fascinating things about the intellectual effects of trying to make a serious gift of one's future to God.

I am discovering that in trying to find God's will and the shape of the Christian life I have begun an adventure so great that its total completion will always be ahead. And this has had a unifying effect on my intellectual life that I had not counted on at all. Years ago the Harvard psychologist Gordon Allport pointed out that the striving for a goal beyond one's reach is thought by many psychologists to be the greatest power for unifying the diverse elements in a personality structure.* Certainly this has seemed to be true in many of the developmental stages of my life.

As an adolescent, for instance, the over-riding purpose of playing basketball affected every part of my living: what I ate, what I drank, how much I slept, and how I did my studies. My whole life was ordered by my desire to play basketball well during high school. I did many other things, but having a single dominant incentive gave me a way to establish my priorities and unify my life during a period which could have been very fragmented. As it turned out, the goal of being a great All American player was beyond my reach. But this only made the unifying effect continue as I played. Because, as Allport pointed out, the *achieving* of a goal is often not nearly as unifying as the *pilgrimage in search of it was.* For instance, the Allies were much more unified in *fighting* the Second World War than when we had won it and should *truly* have had unity.

In trying to commit my life to finding and participating in some of the purposes of Christ, as I can determine them, my energies and abilities are gradually being focused and are working together. I have a point of reference for my learning: what does a book or a new experience in a different field have to say about the world and life as Christ presented them? I have an hypothesis which I can test in all areas of thought and

---

* Allport, Gordon, *Pattern and Growth in Personality.*

relationship. And I sometimes experience a freedom to experiment with and challenge old methods and patterns of teaching the Christian message.

But at other times I push away from God and want to be rich or famous. On such days I have two or more different dominant goals. And I gradually begin to feel split and torn in my attempts to focus all my energies on one or the other. Many times I want to be God's person but want more to be a famous writer some day. And I get caught in a real conflict of motives . . . until I begin again and make a primary commitment of my whole future happiness to Christ—*whatever the outcome may be with regard to my other dominant goals.* Often following such a commitment, I find that paradoxically, I am free to work at my secondary purposes more honestly and creatively, because my ultimate happiness does not depend on succeeding there anymore.

It seems that so many young people today are feeling disintegrated in their lives. They appear to be searching for something, a unifying adventure which will bring into a single focus all of their abilities and energies. I guess I am projecting my own experience on them, because that is what I was looking for all my life: an adventure with a meaning and purpose beyond my grasp—an hypothesis with which to integrate all truths. I guess if I were a professor, I would go and tell them what a relief it is to have found such a unifying adventure in the Christian life . . . because it certainly is.

·+◄◄►►+·

"The staking of a [overall] goal compels the unity of the personality in that it draws the stream of all spiritual activity into its definite direction."[16]

Alfred Adler
*Psychologies of 1930*

"Of course education never is complete, and the process of integration extends throughout life; but that is its fundamental purpose—that out of the chaos which we are at birth order may be fashioned, and from being many we may become one."[17]

William Temple
*Nature, Man and God*

·•✦✦✧✦✦•·

LORD, help me to realize fully the paradoxical freedom that is found through trying to commit all of life to You. Sometimes I am amazed that this commitment has issued in creativity and a freedom to look in all areas for truth, when I had thought it would mean a narrower, restricted intellectual life. Sometimes as I read philosophy and psychology, I am afraid I will find out that You are not real. But I thank You that it is through the strength which comes in this relationship with You that I find the courage to examine even the evidence which might destroy my faith. And for this I am very grateful.

·•✦✦✧✦✦•·

"Jesus then said to the Jews who had believed in him, 'If you continue in my word, you are truly my disciples, and you will know the truth, and the truth will make you free.' "

Jesus Christ
John 8:31,32

# Any Old Bush Will Do

A FRIEND, who is a topflight management consultant and a very sharp Christian layman, went to Europe several years ago. He was excited because he had always wanted to visit the Christian shrines in England and on the continent. He went to Aldersgate Street where John Wesley's "heart was strangely warmed," to Wittenberg and to Rome, where Luther's incisive turnings took place. But as he saw these places, which have become shrines for many Protestant Christians, he was frankly disappointed. He had expected to be inspired and awed, but these were just plain buildings and towns.

As he thought about his disappointment, he realized that these had been just ordinary places when the action had taken place which later made them important. In each case the thing that made these churches and cities shrines was that each was a simple setting in which a man had made a decision concerning God's will for himself—a time when someone turned with his whole life, faced God, and chose Him over "things." The *events which followed* were so significant that people now travel for miles just to see the site where the decision was made.

In considering this I realize that so often I have looked for a special place or dramatic circumstances in which I could do God's will. I remembered a sermon another friend once preached about the places where faith can blossom and lives can be committed. He spoke of Moses and the burning bush, and called the sermon, "Any Old Bush Will Do."

The potential shrines in our lives, then, may not be exciting sites or meetings but rather circumstances in which we run out of our own strength and turn to God, offering Him our futures, whatever the cost. The birth of a deeper transforming faith seems to be the event which melds the decision, the deeds, and the place into a shrine. And for this, *any old bush will do*—any old loneliness or frustration, fear, anxiety, or broken relationship—or any of the outward circumstances in which we find ourselves when we commit our lives to Him. Any of these simple "places" where faith comes alive may one day become for us a Christian shrine—any old house, or kitchen sink, or office chair—wherever you are reading this . . . right now.

··+ 🙦 +··

IN A GARDEN:

". . . I cast myself down I know not how, under a certain figtree, giving full vent to my tears . . . I sent up these sorrowful words; How long? how long, 'tomorrow, and tomorrow'? Why not now? Why not is there this hour an end to my uncleanness?

"So was I speaking, and weeping in the most bitter contrition of my heart, when, lo! I heard from a neighbouring house a voice, as of a boy or girl, I know not, chanting, and oft repeating, 'Take up and read; Take up and read.' Instantly, my countenance altered, I began to think most intently, whether children were wont in any kind of play to sing such words; nor could I remember ever to have heard the like. So checking the torrent of my tears, I arose; interpreting it to be no other than a command from God, to open the book, and read the first chapter I should find. For I had heard of Antony, that coming in during the reading of the Gospel, he received the admonition, as if what was being read, was spoken to him; *Go, sell all that thou hast, and give to the poor, and thou shalt have treasure in heaven, and come and follow me.* And by such oracle he was forthwith converted unto Thee. Eagerly then I returned to the place where Alypius was sitting; for there had I laid the volume of the Apostle, when I arose thence. I seized, opened, and in silence read that section, on which my eyes first fell: *Not in rioting and drunkenness, not in chambering and wantonness, not in strife and envying: but put ye on the Lord Jesus Christ, and make not provision for the flesh,* in concupiscence. No further would I read; nor needed I: for instantly at the end of this sentence, by a light as it were of serenity infused into my heart, all the darkness of doubt vanished away."[18]

Augustine
*The Confessions of St. Augustine*

IN AN OFFICE:

LORD, help me to make this chair and this room a shrine in my own pilgrimage by offering myself to You right now. It is frightening to me to call You "Lord" when I realize that means that I am signing up to be Your servant—to go and do and be according to Your designs, even if they should conflict with my own. Although it is easy for me to say "Lord" most days, sometimes—as right now—I realize the awesome and unconditional response for which You are asking. And I want to say with young Augustine, "not yet Lord." At times like this, I realize why there are so few Christian shrines.

OR ON A HIGHWAY:

"Thus I journeyed to Damascus with the authority and commission of the chief priests. At midday, O king, I saw on the way a light from heaven, brighter than the sun, shining round me and those who journeyed with me. And when we had all fallen to the ground, I heard a voice saying to me in the Hebrew language, 'Saul, Saul, why do you persecute me? It hurts you to kick against the goads.' And I said, 'Who are you, Lord?' And the Lord said, 'I am Jesus whom you are persecuting. But rise and stand upon your feet; for I have appeared to you for this purpose, to appoint you to serve and bear witness to the things in which you have seen me and to those in which I will appear to you, delivering you from the people and from the Gentiles—to whom I send you to open their eyes, that they may turn from darkness to light and from the power of Satan to God, that they may receive forgiveness of sins and a place among those who are sanctified by faith in me.' "

Acts 26:12–18

# "I Love You, Lord, But I Don't Feel Your Presence"

I WAS NERVOUS waiting outside the hotel room for my appointment with Dr. Benton, who was conducting a series of seminars at our church. Finally my turn came.

"I pray regularly," I told him, "but so much of the time I don't feel that God hears me. Not only that, but I don't feel anything much, even when I tell Him I love Him. To pray at times like that seems insincere."

As we talked, I confessed that frequently I didn't feel anything during the communion service either.

The minister leaned back in his chair and thought a minute.

"Are you married?" he asked.

"Yes."

"Do you kiss your wife as you go out the door on the way to work?"

"Yes," I smiled. "Every day."

"Does it give you a great feeling of love every time you kiss her at the doorway?"

I had to admit that sometimes I couldn't even remember whether I had kissed her or not by the time I got to the office.

Dr. Benton identified with my experience, but said that occasionally when he kissed his wife, he was overwhelmed by how much she meant to him as a person. All of those kisses at the door were threads, weaving the fabric of their daily lives into the kind of relationship in which great feelings of love could be experienced naturally and fully when they came. As a Christian, Dr. Benton said that he felt the same way about habits of prayer and worship. Sometimes he did not sense much substance in his feelings for God during his private prayers or at the communion rail, but at other times he was almost overcome by feelings of hope and gratitude to God for His love, acceptance, and for giving him meaning and purpose for his life.

As I was going down the elevator, I could not help smiling when I thought of his analogy about marriage. I remember, when Mary Allen and I were still engaged, arguing with my father about what kind of dog our *children* should have. I recalled the "accidental" touching of our hands in a church pew, and laughing about all of the hamburgers and tuna fish salad we had to eat when we were first married, or even the agony of worrying together about a sick child. And I saw that Dr. Benton was right: a deep loving relationship is woven out of a good many mundane responses which do not *feel* like love at all . . . at the time.

··◆·◆◆·

". . . this fervour is especially characteristic of beginners, and its drying up should be welcomed as a sign that we are getting beyond the first stages. To try to retain it, or to long for its return in the midst of dryness, is to refuse to grow up. It is to refuse the Cross. By our steady adherence to God when the affections are dried up, and nothing is left but the naked will clinging blindly to Him, the soul is purged of self-regard and trained in pure love."[19]

H. A. Hodges
*Unseen Warfare*

·•✦❖✦•·

LORD, help me to need You and want You so consciously and continually that I will turn to You regardless of my religious feelings. Help me to be willing to walk into the problems of today representing You . . . even though I must go without the certainty of a bag of pat answers or perhaps even without any feeling of Your being with me. But so often I am afraid to take real risks without the sense of Your presence. I guess I am praying for faith, Lord, so that I can act on the reality of Your love . . . even when I cannot "see" it with my senses.

·•✦❖✦•·

"And what is faith? Faith gives substance to our hopes, and makes us certain of realities we do not see."

Hebrews 11:1 (NEB)

# Just As I Am . . . When I Give Up the Jug?

ONE EVENING several years ago I was taking a young friend out to dinner. He had just graduated from the university and was going off to enter the Christian ministry the next day. John was one of those fine, clean young men who somehow get through college without scar or blemish from the world. I found him hard to believe, but he was evidently sincere. We had eaten in a cafeteria and were talking about his future when a good-looking young woman sauntered up to our table in a pair of very short shorts, sandals, and one of those brief halter type tops. She was followed by a tiny daughter in a similar outfit. I recognized the woman as a member of the Sunday school class I taught. The class was rather large, and I had seen her only as a member of an audience. A few times I had spoken to her briefly before or after class, but I had definitely noticed her.

Somehow at the cafeteria, however, she looked very "un-Sunday schooly." I introduced her to my young friend as a fellow member of the same Sunday school class, and asked if she would like to join us. She did, and said at once, "There is something I've been wanting to talk to you about for months."

"What's that?"

**69**

"Paul, I think he was a sex deviate."

My young friend's eyes were protruding slightly in horror, and I sort of wished I had not asked.

"Paul who?" I asked, smiling weakly.

She laughed, "You know who I mean, Paul the Apostle."

So we began to talk about Paul's views concerning women and sex. After about forty minutes it was apparent that Paul was not the problem she wanted to talk about, and I told her so.

Her whole attitude changed. She said almost wistfully, "I really believe you've found hope in your faith, and I would honestly like to make this beginning commitment of my life to Christ . . . but I can't do it."

"Why not?" I asked gently.

"Because I've got a personal problem that I can't seem to resolve." She was biting her lips and looking down at a paper napkin she had folded into a small bulky square.

"But that's why Christianity is called 'good news,' " I said, coming on strong. "We can't solve our own basic hangups and separations, and God is offering through the Holy Spirit to furnish us the motivating power to cope with the seemingly impossible situations in life. That's why I'm such a nut about Christianity. I can't promise to change anything. All I can do is to accept His love and grace."

"But," and she hesitated . . . "I don't feel acceptable until I whip this problem."

"Listen, Susan, the old song doesn't say, 'Just as I am when I whip my major problem.' It says, 'Just as I am without *one plea*,' one *promise,* one *guarantee!*"

She looked at me with the strangest dawning look of hope, "Do you really believe that?" She said.

"I'd bet my life on it."

She looked down at her hands for several minutes. "All

right," she said, almost as a challenge, "I'm committing adultery every Thursday night with a man who has a wife and several young children. And I *cannot* quit. Now can I come into your Christian family?"

I just looked at her. I certainly had not expected that. My first conditioned reaction as a Christian churchman would have been to think she is not ready for Christ, or to say something like, "Baby, don't you think you could at least cut down a little?"

Suddenly I realized how phony we Christians are. Of course we *would* expect her to quit committing adultery. We don't mean "just as I am without one plea." We actually mean, "Just as I am when I *promise* implicitly to straighten up and quit my major sins." And this girl had nailed me with her honesty. She had heard the *real* intent of our church's congregational invitation and knew she did not have the strength to meet its requirements—to quit her "sinning." And yet it was her weakness which had brought her toward Christ in the first place.

I thought about Jesus and what He would have done. Then I looked up at her, "Of course, you can commit your life to Christ just as you are," I smiled. "He knows you want to quit seeing this man, and I don't know where else you can ever *hope* to find the security and strength to break up with him. So if you commit your life to Christ right now, then Thursday night, if you find you can't help meeting your friend, take Christ with you in your conscious mind through the whole evening. Ask Him to give you the desire and the strength to break off the relationship."

And she stepped across the stream and became a Christian.

--◦◦◦--

"Sometimes at that moment [in despair] a wave of light breaks into our darkness, and it is as though a voice were saying: 'You are accepted. *You are accepted, accepted* by that which is greater than you . . .'[20]

Paul Tillich
*The Shaking of the Foundations*

"There are many religions which know no divine welcome to the sinner until he has ceased to be one. They would first make him righteous, and then bid him welcome to God. But God in Christ first welcomes him, and so makes him penitent and redeems him. The one demands newness of life; the other imparts it. The one demands human righteousness as the price of divine atonement; the other makes atonement in order to evoke righteousness."[21]

J. S. Whale
*Christian Doctrine*

THANK YOU, LORD, that the guarantee of strength and integrity in this relationship is Yours and not ours. Thank You that Susan sees this, and wants to change because You have accepted her. Thank You that John was there and that he was able to accept Susan in her weakness. Help me to know that I can *promise* You nothing except my *intention* to be Your person. I pray that You will give me the desire and then the strength to put aside those actions which separate me from You and Your other children. But I am very grateful that Your love does not depend on my success in doing so.

". . . when the goodness and loving kindness of God our Savior appeared, he saved us, not because of deeds done by us in righteousness, but in virtue of his mercy . . ."

Titus 3:4,5

"The scribes and Pharisees brought a woman who had been caught in adultery. . . . he stood up and said to them, 'Let him who is without sin among you be the first to throw a stone at her.' "

Jesus Christ
John 8:3–7

# The Love of a Father

TODAY I CAME out of a "tunnel" into a world that seems bright and filled with hope. I had been having the "blahs" again and had been stumbling through my days with a kind of gray feeling. And this morning I wanted to shout at God, "Where did You go? Where are You?" And then I laughed at my own childishness and thought what a thankless job God has taken on—to love us when so often we are not even conscious of Him.

This started me thinking about the idea that God loves us as a "Father." And I wondered why He does. What would this kind of love be like from His perspective. A scene flashed onto the wall of my memory.

It was in the middle of a winter night some years back, shortly after I had seriously tried to give God the key to my future. One of our children had called out in the darkness, "Daaady!" I was surprised since they usually called their mother. But I got up, stumbled into her room and carried her into the bathroom. The only light was a soft red glow shining on her face from the clay mantles in the gas wall heater. I sat her up on the little pottie seat and bent over to hold her so she wouldn't fall. Her head lolled gently to one side and then she would catch herself, but never quite awaken. As I stood there looking at the softness of her face with her eyes closed, and the slightly tousled long blond hair, I was filled with the most amazing sense of love and gratitude to God for that little girl. I kissed her gently on the nose and thought, "Some day you and I will remember this as a time of great closeness." And I could picture us talking about that night when she was a grown girl. But then I realized that *she* would never remember this midnight closeness—because she had been asleep the whole time I was holding her. But even though she was asleep and would not remember these moments, my own love for her had in some way filled and changed my life as I had quietly helped her though a long winter night.

As I tucked her back in bed with a kiss, it struck me that in some sense this might be one of the reasons the whole Christian venture is worth it to God, in light of our amazing lack of awareness of His presence. I saw that He has been with me all along, loving me and helping me in the most mundane ways, even during those long nights of doubt when I have been spiritually asleep, oblivious to His presence. But even then, when I might least have been trying to respond to Him, His love for me may in some way have warmed His life . . . as my love for my little girl did mine.

.·+·◄◄▓►►·+·

"Love seeks one thing only: the good of the one loved. It leaves all the other secondary effects to take care of themselves. Love, therefore, is its own reward."[22]

Thomas Merton
*No Man Is an Island*

.·+·◄◄▓►►·+·

LORD, thank You that while we were yet sinners, while we were asleep to the fact that You were even interested in us, You loved us enough to die for us in Christ. Help us to be able to love those people in our world who cannot respond to others because they are still asleep to the meaning of the kind of love You have given us to pass on.

·⦁·✦⧫❖⧫✦·⦁·

". . . God shows his love for us in that while we were yet sinners Christ died for us."

Paul
Romans 5:8


"This is my commandment, that you love one another as I have loved you."

Jesus Christ
John 15:12

# To Tell the Truth
## (Problem of Integrity No. 2)

"TACT" IS sometimes very difficult for a Christian. We are called on to "speak the truth in love"; and yet I do not believe we are to *worship* being "truthful" in our daily conversations—which truth in any case is often confused with our own *version* of what seems to be true.

Several years ago when I was a new Christian, I decided I would try to be absolutely honest with my wife. We had just moved to a new town and had a good many extra expenses. This transition was making us a little nervous and frantic around the house. In the midst of everything Mary Allen went out and bought a new dress on sale, which she could not return. Buying something new sometimes has a soothing effect on her nerves, and understanding this, I was not too surprised or upset. But when she tried the dress on and asked me how I liked it, I told her I had seen a girl on First Street wearing one just like it that same day. First Street is a very unsavory part of the city. I said the dress was okay, but seeing a cheap-looking girl in one just like it spoiled it for me . . . which was all true. She just glared at me *and never wore the dress*. I was furious. We could not afford it anyway, but to buy the dress and *not wear* it was really terrible.

But I learned something that day. Christian honesty does not mean that I am obligated to express every thought that passes through my mind. I must learn to hear the *real* question someone is asking and answer *that* question, not just the one phrased by the outward words. This was the amazing genius of Jesus' conversation with people. He always saw through their superficial conversation to the real questions they were asking and dealt with them. Mary Allen had been wanting to know, at a deep level, "Am I attractive to you? Is it all right that I impulsively bought this dress just because I feel frantic and dowdy right now? . . . Do you love me?" These were the real "woman questions"; and the true answer to all of them was "yes." But because of my insensitivity, I had answered the superficial question correctly with legalistic honesty—but by so doing I had said "no" to her *real* questions.

Recently I heard a tongue-in-cheek story about a Christian photographer who faced the issue of absolute honesty with his best customer. It seems that an attractive young woman had commissioned him to do an expensive portrait once every ten years. Everything had gone well, but when she was fifty, she was very disappointed with the proofs and more than a little indignant. Charging down to the photographer's studio, she plopped the proofs on his desk. "This picture is not *nearly* as good as the one you made ten years ago!" she said angrily. The photographer looked at the proofs, shook his head thoughtfully for a few seconds, and then nodded sadly, "Well, ma'am, I'm not the man I was ten years ago."

I am not actually suggesting that the photographer did the right thing, but only that he saw the real problem beneath the outward complaint. One might even say that he by-passed the issue. To hear the questions of the heart and answer them is tricky, because of our tendency to avoid the truth when it is painful. But I think this is the risk of trying to move toward the heart of deeper Christian relations. And I believe God wants us to be willing to take risks in trying to love people . . . where they really are.

.+.+#.

". . . I feel the more I know God, that He would sooner we did wrong in loving than never love for fear we should do wrong."[23]

Father Andrew
*The Life and Letters of Father Andrew*

.+.+#.

LORD, help me not to give people my current medical history when they say, "How are you?" in order to "be honest." Help me to know when they are asking real questions and when they are just saying "hello." Give me a sensitive ear, Lord, to hear the secret needs and doubts behind the façade of words I will walk through today. Give me Your perception, Your radar, to locate the hearts of the people along my way this morning.

.+.+#.

"For he knows the secrets of the heart."

Psalm 44:21

"Knowing their thoughts, he said to them . . ."

Matthew 12:25

# The Death and Resurrection
# of the Past

N ANNIE'S DEAD. Aunt Nannie is dead!" I kept saying it over and over to myself and shaking my head. I couldn't believe it, and yet I knew it was true. I had just seen her body at the funeral home.

I felt sick in the lower part of my stomach—empty. My throat was tight. I wanted to cry but could not because of a lifetime of conditioning to "be a man." But I had not expected such a strong reaction. After all, Mother, Dad, and my only brother had all died or been killed over ten years before. And Nannie was only my aunt.

No, she wasn't "only an aunt." She had lived with us for fifteen years during my grade school and high school years. She had helped spoil me and had given me almost continuous approval (or acceptance when she did not approve) all my life. Now she was gone, and a great sadness had come over me. I knew that whatever good God may have for Christians, Nannie would now have. So I wondered why my grief was so deep. But all I could do was drive around the town which had changed so much, and show the children where she had lived. And I knew something was dying inside me.

**80**

That was five months ago, and I finally realized last night why my grief was so deep when Nannie died. I had loved her very much but there was something more. Yesterday we received the initial copy of my first book, *The Taste of New Wine*. I was very excited. I had secretly wanted to write a book since I was a small boy. Mary Allen was excited with me. We didn't think many people would read it, but that did not matter.

I started instinctively for the telephone to call and tell . . . *who?* Then it hit me. Every one who had known me as a child in our home was dead. There was no one to tell who would understand about the dreams and hopes of a little freckle-faced boy who had always tried to look tougher than he was.

When I got in bed that last night, I lay there in the dark and began to weep for the first time in years. A great wave of loneliness came over me. I realized that all the memories of our home had died with Nannie . . . except mine. I was alone with my past. But the flood of grief was a great release.

This morning I can see that last night I stepped across one of the many small streams that separate children from adulthood. And although in one sense I was alone with my past, in another I was not at all—God was with me as a small boy with my hopes and dreams and is with me still. In a sense He and I will always share the memories of the past. In Him not only Nannie but Mother, Dad, and my brother Earle, may in some way that is beyond my understanding still share these memories with me. And in any case I am not alone this morning with my past.

I had never seen before this aspect of Christ's amazing statement, "I am with you alway, even unto the end of the world"—that His presence is really the thread which runs through the memories in a Christian's life, holding the years together, giving them unity of meaning like a string of pearls.

Without His continuing presence with each of us, fear, separation, and death would scatter the Christian family in the wind. And although at times I am still lonely, God's presence and Christ's promises help me not to feel alone when I face my family's death . . . and my own.

···❄···

" 'The paths of glory lead but to the grave'—whether the 'glory' be the conspicuous achievements (or perhaps only the conspicuousness) of the 'great,' or the modest successes, or the 'quaint deeds' of ordinary men. Not long ago I had occasion to visit a small church in a small town in Virginia where my father was pastor some fifty years ago and where I spent an important part of my boyhood. My father was quiet and modest, a man of remarkable intelligence, humor, and charm and of quite extraordinary goodness, and I found that he was vividly remembered by the oldest members of the church. But the number of these is small and becomes smaller as each year passes, and quite soon no one at all will remember him. His name will be read for a while—as on a window in the church which they have dedicated to his memory—but the name will mean no more to those who read it than most of the names on the plaques and portraits of old buildings mean to us. Not only will he be silent, as he has been for nearly forty years, but he will no longer speak, for there will be no one to hear him. He will be forgotten. Here is perhaps the supreme pathos of human life—not that we die only but that any real and living memory of us must die too. Unless God is to raise us from death, it is in the end as though we had never been. Our dead have perished leaving no trace except our sad, if grateful, remembrance of them—and in the final reckoning no trace at all.

"Death is the 'last enemy,' and no man, however strong willed and defiant, no matter how stoical or wise, can wrest the final victory from its hands. Our only hope is in God. 'Save us, Lord, or we perish'—perish finally and utterly, along with all we love and treasure."[24]

John Knox
*Life in Jesus Christ*

·+ ✦❊❧✦ +·

LORD, thank You for not only healing the bad memories of the past through forgiveness but for preserving the good ones in the memory bank of Your mind. Thank You for Your awareness of our efforts and strivings, which sometimes seems to be the only thing that gives meaning when we fail. But thank You most of all that You have promised to take our hands when they can no longer reach out to You, and lead us through the doorway between death and life.

·+ ✦❊❧✦ +·

"Lo! I tell you a mystery. We shall not all sleep, but we shall all be changed, in a moment, in the twinkling of an eye, at the last trumpet. For the trumpet will sound, and the dead will be raised imperishable, and we shall be changed. For this perishable nature must put on the imperishable, and this mortal nature must put on immortality. When the perishable puts on the imperishable, and the mortal puts on immortality, then shall come to pass the saying that is written: 'Death is swallowed up in victory, O death, where is thy victory? O death, where is thy sting?' The sting of death is sin, and the power of sin is the law. But thanks be to God, who gives us the victory through our Lord Jesus Christ."

I Corinthians 15:51–58

# It's the Little Things Which Count

WHAT'S so horrible about leaving the toilet seat up in the middle of the night?" I was furious and defensive. I knew that her reaction at breakfast was far too heavy for the nature of the complaint. That made me mad too . . . and frustrated. It seemed as if everything I did anymore bugged her—innocent mistakes like leaving the shower head at "on" over the bathtub, or forgetting to close the closet door in our bedroom.

I work very hard, spend a lot of time with our family, and try to be generous as a provider. These petty complaints over a few mechanical omissions which were totally accidental, from my perspective, seemed unreasonable, and I was beginning to suspect that I had a nagging wife. But as I drove to work the realization came back that—as bad as it was—the incident the night before was not as big as her anger. (This always means that the present argument is not the real one.) So I began to try to find out the true cause of this rash of getting mad about "little things." It was obvious that something I was doing or being was causing her to run up her red flag.

When the dust settled during the next couple of days, she was able to tell me, "Honey, what these careless things you keep doing *really* say to me is that you don't care enough about me to make an effort to stop doing things which make me mad and frustrated." She stopped and then went on, "I guess I keep waiting for you to remember, and when you don't, I get madder."

"I really *do* care . . ." I started, in defense of myself. But I stopped, because I know that we *do* what we unconsciously want to do in life. I may protest to high heaven that I honestly want to remember things and just cannot. However, I have learned that this is often a deceitful trick the mind plays on itself. Many psychologists have understood that we seldom forget something we *really* want to do unless we have a reason that is hidden . . . often from ourselves.* A golfing enthusiast may forget to take his wife shopping, but he is not likely to forget a golf partner. A young man in love with his girl friend is not apt to forget to pick her up for a date— even if he does forget to do his homework assignment and mow the yard the same weekend. Although I am terribly forgetful about many things, I did not forget a single basketball practice or game during the twenty years I participated in that sport.

Remembering this made me realize that I was evidently not interested in helping Mary Allen's feelings of discomfort and frustration—at least not interested enough to remember certain little common courtesies. Why not, I wondered? I love her and want to be a good husband. And I feel certain that God would have me *at least* care for her needs and comfort with common courtesy.

Then I remembered. Several weeks before I had been feeling especially romantic. And she had been feeling especially tired. I had interpreted her tiredness as a purposeful rejection

---

* Sigmund Freud, *A General Introduction to Psychoanalysis* (New York: Washington Square Press, Inc.), see excellent discussion on the "psychology of errors" in Part I.

and was particularly furious when she claimed later that she had not gotten my signals. I remembered smoldering and thinking, "If she really loved me, she would always be sensitive to my needs!"

So that was my problem. The world was centered in *me* again. But being too proud and "too good a Christian" to set out consciously to punish her for hurting my pride, I repressed the feelings. And I got back at her subtly and unconsciously by forgetting things which hurt her pride—things that made her feel the way I had felt: that she was not loved enough for me to think about her needs and comfort.

And do you know what? When I realized that the problem had started in *me* weeks before and it was that most pervasive sin of self-centeredness, my average improved tremendously in remembering the shower head, the toilet seat, and the closet door.

·+◄◊║◊►+·

"For there is only one sin, and it is characteristic of the whole world. It is the self-will which prefers 'my' way to God's—which puts 'me' in the centre where only God is in place. It pervades the universe. It accounts for the cruelty of the jungle, where each animal follows its own appetite, unheeding and unable to heed any general good. It becomes conscious, and thereby tenfold more virulent in man—a veritable Fall indeed."[25]

William Temple
*Readings in St. John's Gospel*
·+◄◊║◊►+·

THANK YOU, GOD, for showing me again that so many of my complaints about other people could be stopped if I could only see my sin. I am amazed at the way I can hide my true motives even from myself. But I am grateful for finding out this morning another of the deceitful maneuvers my ego uses to protect the "fine man" image . . . when a consciousness of my true intentions would destroy it.

·+·❀·+·

"The heart is deceitful above all things, and desperately corrupt; who can understand it? 'I the Lord search the mind and try the heart, to give to every man according to his ways, according to the fruit of his doings.' "

Jeremiah 17:9,10

# Squelching a Word of Love

"THAT WAS a great job, Keith!" The man who was speaking is a person whom I deeply respect and love. I had just given a talk in our church, and he was enthusiastically and sincerely affirming me.

"Thanks, but I'm afraid I was too direct," I replied. "I was tired and felt a little hostile." He looked at me strangely, and I went into the educational wing to get ready for church school.

While walking away, I realized what I had done. I had very subtly and unintentionally devalued him as a person. He was trying to tell me that I had done a good job, and he had really meant it. But instead of thanking him for his affirmation, I had told him in effect, "Actually, you aren't really very smart. I heard some negative things about my talk which you didn't hear." Although I had not said that, I saw that my negative reply had in some way rejected him and his kindness in complimenting me in the first place.

Thinking about what had happened, I realized how often I turn people off when they try to say something nice to me. If I happened to make a high score on an examination in college, for instance, and someone said, "Congratulations," I might have laughed and come back with something cute like, "As

88

much time as I spent studying for that one, an orangutan would have done well." I seemed to turn attention away from their attempts to affirm me . . . thinking somehow that I was being humble.

But now I am beginning to see that instead of humility, this inability to accept praise or affirmation is really an insidious form of pride and insecurity. Further, it represents a completely thoughtless attitude toward the needs of the one trying to offer the congratulations. If a person is sincere with his compliments, he is going out on a limb to identify with me. He is reaching out to say, "I, too, feel as you do or appreciate life as you do." Or, "In some sense we are brothers or I would not have responded to what you said." But my reply of supposed humility has turned the attention *away* from him and toward me and my cleverness. I have devalued his love by joking or saying in effect, "No, we are *not* alike, because you misinterpreted my performance." Or, "Your perception is faulty." Or, "If you are like me, you are really a dummy, for any dolt could have done what I have."

It is clear to me now that with all my apparent willingness, as a Christian, to love other people, I fail to love them when I refuse to hear their attempts to love me. I suppose I reject their love because I'm afraid it is unreal, and I cannot risk being hurt—in case they do not mean it—or sometimes I evidently want to appear humble, if they do mean it. So I protect myself from being hurt or from looking proud by dismissing as insignificant any attempts people make to say affirming things to me. Never before had I realized fully the negative, squelching effect of refusing to accept another's kind words.

Since making these discoveries, I am going to try to look people in the eye and say simply and warmly, "Thank you," if they try to say something positive to me. At a deep level I know that anything worthwhile I have is from God. And somehow, by letting people express positive feelings to me through a handshake and a few words, I think something is completed in the attempt to communicate the love of God in human terms.

··+◄◄░▓►+··

"Words and magic were in the beginning one and the same thing, and even today words retain much of their magical power. By words one of us can give to another the greatest happiness or bring about utter despair . . . Words call forth emotions and are universally the means by which we influence our fellow creatures. Therefore let us not despise the use of words. . . ."[26]

Sigmund Freud
*A General Introduction to
Psychoanalysis*

··+◄◄░▓►+··

THANK YOU, GOD, that You are willing to receive my stumbling and often half-sincere attempts to praise You. Since You showed us in Christ that it is important for us to be able to receive, please give us the grace we need to do so. I am grateful that You take these praises of mine seriously rather than rejecting me with a denial or a joke, which would leave me alone and sorry I tried. Help me to learn how to love. But O Lord, give me the security to risk *receiving* from other people . . . love, which I fear may not be real.

··+◄◄░▓►+··

IT IS HARD TO RECEIVE:

"Peter said to him, 'You shall never wash my feet.' Jesus answered him, 'If I do not wash you, you have no part in me.' Simon Peter said to him, 'Lord, not my feet only but also my hands and my head!' "

John 13:8,9

# A Widow's "Might"

THIS WEEK in a small group we were talking about how we might find a place of lasting importance in our community in which to participate in God's work. We began by examining those things we were presently doing which involved helping people outside of our own families. Some of the usual church and civic activities were mentioned. Then we came to a perky, bright little white-haired lady named Jane who is eighty years old. She had been a registered nurse all her adult life, and we had all been affected by her frankness, vitality, and her love of God.

Jane said, "I've found that there is a terrible problem among the bedridden old people in this town. Many of them suffer constantly because they are constipated, and there is no one to give them the proper nursing care of an enema." And so this dear, cheery little saint has been going around among the poor giving the very sick old men and women in our town a fantastic number of enemas for Christ's sake.

We were embarrassed and tried not to smile when she first began to talk; but as she continued, I quit being embarrassed and started hearing what this remarkable woman was saying to us. I drew her out and asked her how she had started nursing people in her spare time for no charge.

*91*

She thought a minute and then smiled, as she remembered. "When I was a red-haired young nurse," she began, "I got very upset at the hospital in which I was working. They would turn poor people away who could not show evidence of financial capability. This bothered me a lot because some of them had no place to go." It was apparent that she had been very angry. Jane went on to tell us how she had prayed about what to do. As a result she had opened her small home to some of the destitute sick women, finally filling it with cots and beds. Some of her patients were Catholics, some were Protestants, and others were non-Christians. They had all sorts of different cultural and social backgrounds, but all were sick. She nursed them when she got off work.

Not having much money, Jane soon spent all she had. One morning she sat down on the front step and cried into a $30.00 milk bill, which she had no way of paying. Having told God that she could not put these sick people out in the street, she had no idea where to go for help. She suddenly remembered a fiery young Episcopal priest (who was to become one of the outstanding bishops in the church). Putting on her coat she rushed to his office. She was very frightened—afraid he would not even listen. But she got in and told him her story—how in obedience to that which she felt God had revealed to her in her prayer, she had opened her house to all kinds of sick people. And she had spent everything on their care.

The big priest looked at her with a twinkle in his eye, and said with mock seriousness, "Why have you got all these Baptists and Methodists and Catholics? Maybe you shouldn't be in the Episcopal Church."

"I am *not* leaving my church!" she said with tears coming to her eyes. "And *you* should help me!"

"What in the world do you want me to do?" he asked with a questioning gesture.

Jane had no idea how much to ask for, so she plopped the unpaid milk bill into his hand, and said, "Well, you can begin by paying the milk bill." And he did.

Years later, that bishop completed an amazing career of service and influence. Most people never knew that the mammoth Christian medical center he had promoted—for Baptists, Methodists, and *all* kinds of people—might never have been built except for the vision he had seen in the simple obedience of a poor little red-headed nurse . . . who was trying to love her Lord and the people around her.

··+·▪❖▪·+··

". . . The really important thing is that in those early days the pagans saw in Christianity and in the Church a power that could cope with and mend the human situation. They saw in Christianity a power which they did not possess—and they wanted it. It will always be true that the outsider will have no use for an alleged faith which is demonstrably ineffective. Long ago Nietzschze, the atheist philosopher, issued the challenge: 'Show me that you are redeemed and then I will believe in your Redeemer.' The greatest converting influence of all is a life which clearly and obviously is possessed of a power which can cope with the human situation in all its problems, in all its tragedy, and in all its pain."[27]

William Barclay
*Turning to God*

··+·▪❖▪·+··

LORD, I am glad that You made a moving drama of the Christian life instead of a study course in abstract philosophy. Thank You that the role You have given me is important to You as the Author—however insignificant I may feel as I look at the "great ones" in the world's eyes. I am grateful that the "size" of our outward results does not seem as important to You as the depth of the commitment our behavior reveals. Help me to "commit it all" today.

"And he sat down opposite the treasury, and watched the multitude putting money into the treasury. Many rich people put in large sums. And a poor widow came, and put in two copper coins, which make a penny. And he called his disciples to him, and said to them, 'Truly, I say to you, this poor widow has put in more than all those who are contributing to the treasury. For they all contributed out of their abundance; but she out of her poverty has put in everything she had, her whole living.' "

Jesus Christ
Mark 12:41–44

# Mixed Motives—A Problem
# for the Intense
## (Problems of Integrity No. 3)

Mommy, i'm not sure if I am being nice to these people because I like them or because I believe it will make them think I'm a neat kid. And it worries me. Should I quit being so friendly?"

The lady who was showing me this passage from a letter was puzzled. It was from her young teenage daughter who was away at camp for the summer. The mother said that she had not worried about such things when she was a girl and asked me what I thought about the letter.

Smiling a little to myself, I realized that I could have written a similar letter at many different times in my life. The problem—of mixed motives—has given me fits in several different ways. Those of us who have a deep need to be accepted, and for whom acceptance as a child was subtly contingent on our "being good," may have more trouble with motivational nit-picking than other people. Sometimes in school, I remember worrying about whether I was thoughtful to other kids because I meant it or because by being friendly to them I would likely be elected to class offices. Although I

**95**

knew at some level that both motives were there and that both were pretty natural, I wanted to be *sure my* motives were right—like the little girl in the letter.

When I became a Christian, this occasional compulsive need to have pure motives took an especially insidious form, which brought the whole business to a head. Beginning to witness in other churches as a layman, I wondered sometimes if I were going because I wanted to tell people about God . . . or about me. This worried me, since I really wanted to be God's person and to do His will. On one occasion I almost called a minister and canceled a meeting because I wasn't sure if I were going for God or for Keith. But having put off contacting him until it was very late, I went ahead and drove to the church—knowing that my motives were definitely mixed. Before I spoke that night, I prayed silently that God would use me "if You can use a man as full of himself as I am." After I started speaking, I forgot all about my motives.

Several days later a man who attended the meeting came to my office. He said that he had been desperate and had almost lost hope, but as a result of attending the session that night had decided to give life another try. After he left, I sat thinking about what had happened.

In the first place, my desire to keep my motives spotless and pure had almost kept me from helping a man who was really desperate. I saw how totally self-centered this "keeping myself righteous" is. It constitutes a strange kind of Christian idolatry—I was worshiping clean motives. Keeping them spotless was more important somehow than going ahead with mixed motives and letting God possibly help someone through me.

In the second place, it came crashing home to me that my motives are *always* mixed to some degree—and that most likely they always will be in this life. So that for me, the leap of faith in witnessing for Christ is to go, knowing my needs for attention, but taking the risk that I will speak for Him instead of for myself. I must go in faith, praying that God will use me in spite of my self-centeredness.

In fact, after all these years, I simply pray that God will free me to point over my shoulder to Him. Because when it comes right down to it, all I have to tell about is what I have seen and heard of Him—how He is helping me to find freedom, occasionally to love other people, and even to accept myself with my mixed motives.

·+·❈❀·+·

"What can we take with us on this journey to we do not know where? What we must take is the knowledge of our own unending ambiguous motives. . . .

"The voice that we hear over our shoulders never says, 'First be sure that your motives are pure and selfless and then follow me.' If it did, then we could none of us follow. So when later the voice says, 'Take up your cross and follow me,' at least part of what is meant by 'cross' is our realization that we are seldom any less than nine parts fake. Yet our feet can insist on answering him anyway, and on we go, step after step, mile after mile. How far? How far?"[28]

Frederick Buechner
*The Magnificent Defeat*

·+·❈❀·+·

DEAR LORD, help me not to be a Christian Pharisee who is more interested in being ethical than in loving You and Your people. Be with the little girl who wrote the letter to her mother, and help her to understand that sometimes she will have to risk her motives in order to do anything good. Give us both the courage to follow You even if it means taking the risk, as You did, of being misunderstood. I want to resist phoniness . . . yet without wallowing in the problems of motivation. It all seems very complex, and sometimes I do not even understand my behavior after the fact. So I am offering myself and my subtly mixed motives to You, asking that You will take me beyond such self-centered preoccupations into Your loving perspective.

⋅⋅✦◀✧▶✦⋅⋅

"I do not understand my own actions. For I do not do what I want, but I do the very thing I hate . . . Wretched man that I am! Who will deliver me from this body of death? Thanks be to God through Jesus Christ our Lord! . . ."

Romans 7:15,24,25

# Motivation for Christian Education:
# A Changed Life

H ow can a church leader motivate people even to come
out to *hear* the gospel, much less to become Christians?"
This question seems to be implicit in every leadership meeting I attend. I have found a single recurring answer echoing
down the years. For many people there is only one universally
effective way to interest people in Christianity—and that is to
expose them to a person with whom they can identify, a
person who is finding hope and meaning in Christ in his own
life. For years I was a little hesitant about the idea of new
Christians trying to influence other people before they really
understood some of the implications of the gospel. However,
not long ago something happened that made me rethink this
whole matter.

While on a speaking trip in another state, I was restless
and tired. Feeling phony and miserable, I did not want
to speak to this particular group. How could I possibly project hope and purpose concerning the Christian life?

Waiting my turn to speak, I looked out over those hundreds
of strange faces. I wondered if anyone else had come to this
meeting unwillingly . . . and could not shake loose from the

**99**

slough of self-pity and the frustration of not being able to control his circumstances. But after I had finished speaking, I found myself still standing before the lectern, sort of hesitating. Finally, I heard myself saying something I had never said before—and was a little embarrassed because it sounded like some kind of gimmick: "You know, I have the strangest feeling that I came all this way to talk to one of you who may be going through some of the same feelings of frustration and self-pity I am. And if you think you are the person, I would like to meet you after this session."

As I sat down, I mentally kicked myself in the backside. "Why did you say a stupid thing like that? These people will think you are some kind of a kook." But it was too late.

After the program a large number of men came to extend the courtesy of greeting the speakers. As the line came by, I forgot all about my closing remarks until a short, heavy-set man with glasses and black wavy hair walked up to me. When he shook my hand, he gripped it with great intensity. I looked into his eyes and saw a couple of tears start down his cheeks. Leaning forward, I said quietly, "Say, if you have a minute I'd like to talk to you." He nodded. I pointed over to a corner and said I would be there in a few minutes.

As soon as I could break loose, I went to him. "What are you doing here?" I asked him.

"This is the damnedest thing that ever happened to me. I am an attorney and travel a lot. Although we belong to this denomination," and he nodded toward the group still clustered around the speaker's platform, "it hasn't really meant anything to me in years. I certainly never planned to come to this meeting. As a matter of fact . . ." and here he stopped and looked at me a little uneasily. But then he went on, "As a matter of fact, I have a mistress in this town and was coming to see her—though I was supposedly on a business trip. For weeks I have been feeling very guilty. I wanted out of this relationship, but couldn't seem to break it off. Well, anyway, when I got out of my car a block from this church in front of her apartment, who should come charging up to clap me on the back but three guys from my home church. I almost fainted as one of them asked, 'What are you doing here, Joe?' 'I, uh . . . I'm just passing through,' I lied, scared to death they were going to see the guilt written all over me.

" 'Hey, great. We're just going down to hear some Christian businessmen speak. You've gotta come with us.' And I was afraid to say no for fear I'd somehow give myself away.

"But as I sat there in the meeting and heard you speak about a new start in life—a life with purpose and meaning, I was amazed. I had given up on having any purpose and meaning and had been filled with self-pity. I had no idea what to do. Then you stood up there and looked squarely at me and said what you did, and I knew that I was the one." He stopped talking and looked at me.

"Listen," I said, not really knowing what to do since I had to catch a plane. "We haven't much time. Would you like to commit your whole future to God, including the relationship with this woman?"

He just stood there biting his lips, and finally said, "Boy, I *sure would!*"

"All right. There are a couple of things involved in beginning, as I understand it. One is to confess that you really want your own way more than God's; and if you can do that, then ask God, as He is revealed in Christ, to come into your own inner life and show you how to live for Him . . . and then give Him permission to make you want to."

In a prayer, standing in the corner of that huge church, Joe made a new beginning. I pointed out that Christianity was not a "ticket to heaven" but a way of life that starts now and transcends death, and that all he had done with me was to make a bare beginning—now he had to begin to learn to live again.

I heard my name called and noticed that the people who were to drive me to the airport were looking at their watches. Hating to leave this man, I said, "Hey, listen, Joe, I'll make a deal with you. I'll pray for you every morning for a month if you will pray for me. If you want to go on after that, write me a card and say, 'You're on for another month,' and I'll stay with you a month at a time from now on."

Joe was in tears as he shook my hand. I hated to leave but had to. Glancing at my watch, I saw that the whole interview had lasted about twelve minutes.

When I got home from that trip at the end of the month, there was a letter from Joe. He had begun to live for God. Things looked great. He had started by breaking off the relationship with his mistress. Already it was hard, but he was going to try for another month if I would stick with him.

Well, I knew old Joe was in for some real adjustments. And as the months went by, I was amazed at the way God was getting hold of this man. He began reading the Scriptures and all the books he could get his hands on about living the Christian life, and he began going to his church and having long talks with his minister. Joe began to see his self-centeredness and changed his behavior toward his family and friends in the little southwestern town of a few thousand in which he lived. During all this time I had not seen Joe or talked to him. All he knew was that someone he had met one day was praying for him at 6:30 every morning.

About a year later Joe wrote and said he had told a few people about what was happening to him, but he did not feel they understood him. If I would come to his church, he said he would get these people together for a discussion about living for Christ as a businessman.

This was a very busy time in my life. But I had gotten Joe into this, and the circumstances were so unusual that I thought the least I could do would be to go and visit with the little group to which he was trying to witness. So I went.

I got in just in time for the meeting. Joe met my plane and was very excited as we drove to his church. He said he was sure glad I was there, because several people in town had come right out and asked him what had happened to his life. Since I had never written any books or articles, his friends would know me only as "a friend of Joe's." As we arrived at the church, the minister said that he was glad I'd come and that Joe had really helped him personally. By this time we were a few minutes late. We went through a door at one end of the church to meet the friends who were curious about Joe's life. I stopped for several seconds . . . looking into the faces of over 800 people crowded into every corner and aisle of that church and adjoining rooms.

I realized in that moment that all of the promoted programs and Christian education plans in the world will be virtually worthless to motivate people to become Christians —unless they see some ordinary person like Joe who is finding hope and a new way to live in Christ. And then they will listen.

·+ ✦✿✦ +·

"The most pragmatic of reasons for seeing that Christ is the most dependable of realities is that of changed human lives. When we consider Saul of Tarsus on the road to Damascus, we are in the realm of the empirical as contrasted with the merely speculative. Saul said it was the Living Christ who had met him, and the person who seeks to deny this is confronted with the fact of a permanent change in Saul's character. We cannot, of course, know whether a man is lying when he says 'I believe,' because belief is intrinsically internal and personal, but the evidence of changed lives is something which other people can observe. In Saul's case the change was so radical that it led to the production of some of the finest literature of the world, a literature which would not have been produced apart from the crucial encounter.

"The evidence of lives changed by contact with Christ is so abundant that the full story can never be told; it is, indeed, of a kind not matched anywhere in any culture. The changed lives have come about, not primarily by a set of ideas or by acceptance of a doctrine, but by commitment to a Person."[29]

D. Elton Trueblood
*A Place to Stand*

LORD, we have somehow lost the art of living in our attempts to educate people into the Kingdom of God. Sometimes I have reduced Your Way into a study program "about" the faith of the church. At other times I have tried the emotional techniques of psychology and industry to motivate people to participate in the life of Your church. Help me, Lord, to spend time with persons, time in which we can discover together how to live our days and nights for You. Help me to learn again the amazing motivating power of lives which are in the process of discovery and change. Give me something of the patience and vision You had in spending two-thirds of your ministry with a group of twelve.

"And as he [Jesus] was getting into the boat, the man who had been possessed with demons begged him that he might be with him. But he refused, and said to him, 'Go home to your friends, and tell them how much the Lord has done for you, and how he has had mercy on you.' And he went away and began to proclaim in the Decapolis how much Jesus had done for him; and all men marveled."

Mark 5:18–20

# The Servant

LAST WEEK I was very busy trying to get what seemed like a thousand things done before leaving for a three-day speaking trip on the East Coast. There hadn't been time to prepare my talks so I was under a lot of pressure when a friend, a fine Christian woman, called. A couple she knew was having marital problems. "They might call you," she said, "because they could not agree on either a minister or a psychiatrist." But my friend thought it crucial that I see them if at all possible.

It seems that the majority of the people I've counseled with lately have had marital problems. Even though I was dead tired, I agreed to talk with them, hoping they wouldn't call. But sure enough at almost midnight the telephone rang. The man called me "Reverend" Miller (in what I thought was a condescending tone).

"Keith Miller," I said with some definiteness. "I am a layman."

"I'd like to make an appointment to see you," he said without any details or preliminary remarks. Just when I started to ask who was calling, it occurred to me that he must be the husband of the couple having troubles. He proceeded to set up the appointment. I was too tired and off balance to say, "Wait just a minute, friend." Besides I realized the man was under pressure and had probably put off calling all evening. So the appointment was made for one o'clock the following day at our house.

I was irritated since this meant driving five miles from my writing hideout in the middle of the day. Asking myself, "What kind of a Christian are you if you can't help another human being in trouble?" helped some. But it made me mad that this guy was treating me like some sort of a hired hand. I was only seeing him as a friend, with no intention of charging him as a counselor. So I prayed to be open to the man, and I was (at least consciously) by the time I got home the next day at 12:30. The telephone rang at 1:10 and the man said, "Something has come up and I won't be able to make it to your house." I started to tell him he could just forget it, but then it occurred to me that he might be avoiding the conference purposely. And from what my friend had said, this man could be in serious trouble. So I agreed to see him the following day.

We had a good visit, but it was apparent that their marital problems were severe. By that time my schedule was really pressing. Not long after the husband left, his wife called and after a long conversation, she asked for an appointment. Knowing how hard it is to wait when things seem to be closing in on you, I agreed to see her at 11:00 the following morning.

I rushed home at 10:55 to find that the woman had just called and left word: something had come up and she was not going to be able to come. I was *furious!* Three days had been fouled up by these people. They didn't even have the courtesy to consider how much inconvenience I was going through for them. I wanted to call and tell them that one of their problems was "self-centeredness." And further I wanted to inform them that I was very busy myself . . . and then it hit me: how important I must think I am if a thing like this can make me as mad as it did. Here were two people in the agony of struggling to keep their home together—with no telling what other complications—and I was incensed that they were treating me like a common servant . . . when that is what I have committed my life to be: a servant to Christ and His suffering people. But my behavior told me that secretly I must want to be treated like a big shot writer and counselor.

···❖···

"For the self-flattery of our nature is very subtle and few can discern it. Secretly it pursues only its own ends, though meanwhile its outward conduct is such, that it seems to us we have but the single aim of pleasing God, though in actual fact this is not so . . . So if a man does not watch himself well, he may begin some activity with the sole purpose of pleasing the Lord, but later, little by little, introduce into it a self-interest, which makes him find in it also a satisfaction of his own desires, and this to such an extent that the will of God becomes completely forgotten."[30]

Lorenzo Scupoli
*Unseen Warfare*

"In renunciation it is not the comforts, luxuries and pleasures that are hard to give up. Many could forego heavy meals, a full wardrobe, a fine house, et cetera; it is the ego that they cannot forego. The self that is wrapped, suffocated in material things—which include social position, popularity, and power—is the only self they know and they will not abandon it for an illusory new self . . . which they may never attain."[31]

Mahatma Gandhi
*Ghandi, His Life and Message
for the World*

···❖···

FORGIVE ME, LORD, and help me not to look for the respect and acclaim of people but to be willing to die to my self-concern enough to accept them just as they are. For the good of this couple I do not think I should be a doormat, and I will be firm in any future contact with them with regard to their keeping appointments if they want help. But I see that the worst problem is mine—not theirs. Change my attitude, Lord, to one of a servant.

·⊹+✦⊱⊰✦+⊹·

"And Jesus called them to him and said to them, 'You know that those who are supposed to rule over the Gentiles lord it over them, and their great men exercise authority over them. But it shall not be so among you; but whoever would be first among you must be your servant, and whoever would be first among you must be slave of all. For the Son of man also came not to be served but to serve, and to give his life as a ransom for many.' "

Jesus Christ
Mark 10:42–45

# Temptation: A Strong Wind for a Flickering Flame

TEMPTATION IS a strange experience for me. I want to be God's person. But I also have some deep human needs for approval, affection, and the satisfaction of strong physical and emotional drives. When wrestling with a specific temptation, I seem to change into a different person inside. I have a kind of channel vision and only see the object of my resentment, greed, or lust. All else is blotted out. I am no longer the smiling, friendly Christian, but instead am an intense and sweating stranger—yet not a stranger, for I know this one so well. Reason waits outside the door of temptation for me. I argue against my conscience and dazzle myself with agile rationalizations. By that time the battle is usually lost.*

Of course, sometimes there are long periods of peace and productivity when all the dragons appear to be dead. But then, one day when I am seemingly in good control of my emotions, I am suddenly in the midst of temptation. My

---

* Thomas à Kempis pointed out in the *Imitation of Christ* that the only time to stop temptation is at the first point of recognition. If one begins to argue and engage in a hand to hand combat, temptation almost always wins the day.

**110**

senses are alive to the object of my resentment or my desire. I am practically engulfed in the urge to surrender to my inclination—to glorify my desires above everything—the instant they are born. And sweeping away reason, goodness, God's will, caution, and potential guilt—I succumb.

People who have not had this experience as Christians would make poor counselors for men like me. I know you may say that I am weak. And of course that is the truth. I am weak. But my question is, "What does a weak, yet sincerely committed, Christian do when temptation gets through his blockers and tackles him with a crippling jolt?"

My reactions have been varied. Almost always I feel inadequate and do not like myself. I shy away from prayer, feeling that somehow I could have resisted longer and not succumbed. It is strange, but because of my pride, I always think I could have conquered. But this notion rests on the dubious idea that if I am truly committed to Christ, I *can* control all my actions with reason and determination—if I will just try hard enough.

The truth about the Christian life seems to be, however, that *no one* bats a thousand in facing temptation. As a matter of fact, most of the saints felt that their averages were pretty low. We can improve our performance, and I thank God that this is so. But evidently in this life we will always have the occasional experience of succumbing to temptation. The sad truth is that much of the time I am too weak to resist, and my failure is simply a hard cold fact with which I must live. I have to come to God with the horribly uncomfortable feeling of failure. And finally, with no excuses, I force myself to my knees before Him in confession, asking for restoration to a state of usefulness and self-acceptance by His grace.

I thank Him that this process is what the gospel is all about —the forgiveness of the glorification of our desires and pride to a position above everything, including Him. And asking Him for a new set of controlling desires, I thank Him for the miracle of forgiveness and the strange new start He can give me. I pull myself to my feet, brush the caked spiritual mud from my clothes and walk into another day as His child.

·•◄❊►•·

"First don't dwell on yourself, do not say: 'How could I be such as to allow and suffer it?' This is a cry of proud self-opinion. Humble yourself and, raising your eyes to the Lord say and feel: 'What else could be expected of me, O Lord, weak and faulty as I am.' "[32]

Lorenzo Scupoli
*Unseen Warfare*

"I resolve to meet evil courageously, but when even a small temptation cometh, I am in sore straits. That which seemeth trifling sometimes giveth rise to a grievous temptation; and when I think myself to be secure, and least expect it, I am overcome by a light breath."[33]

Thomas à Kempis
*The Imitation of Christ*

·•◄❊►•·

DEAR LORD, I know it must have broken Your heart to realize that even those of us who follow You would get carried away and crush the people around us, trying to satisfy our hungers for attention and power.

Help me not to kid myself about my real needs and desires and cloak them with phony righteous motives or plead "weakness" as an excuse for succumbing to temptation. I realize that I am capable of almost any sin. Give me the courage to face You more realistically. I pray that You will make those things which are creative, beautiful, and constructive so attractive to me that I will run toward them . . . away from the crippling world of inordinate self-indulgence.

And Lord, thank you for indicating that You believe a man should be forgiven more than once.

····••

"Then Peter came up and said to him, 'Lord, how often shall my brother sin against me, and I forgive him? As many as seven times?' Jesus said to him, 'I do not say to you seven times, but seventy times seven.'"

Matthew 18:21,22

# The Need to Be Included

THIS WEEK two people have called to ask us for details about a party which is being given by some good friends of ours. In each case we laughed and said that we were sorry we couldn't help them because we were not invited. They were very embarrassed, and we thought the whole thing was funny. In any case, we had another regular commitment to a group of Christians on that night and could not have accepted.

But then, when I was alone in my office, I found myself wondering why they did not invite us, since both couples who called fit our "category" for invitations. And one was not particularly close to the host couple at all. I felt all this even though I realized our friends knew about our other commitment. The insecurities of my childhood came scampering back across the years to make me miserable.

How strange this experience is. I wouldn't trade our Christian life and friends and the meaning we are finding together in Christ for any other way of living we have known—especially the driving, party-filled life. And yet when the first "sounds of the music" reach my ears across the night, I am sometimes gripped by my "inner child of the past" who tells me I am being left out of life. And I realize that it is this built-in incompleteness which keeps me from congratulating myself about my self-sufficiency in Christ, and makes me turn again to God as a child.

In counseling during the past few years, and in my own experience, I have come to see how universal and exaggerated the need to be accepted can be. The desire can be strongly activated even when one is not particularly interested in the event in question.

Some years ago when our children were much younger, we all had been out on a family picnic. When we came home, we were very tired. One of the little girls ran in and asked me to unbutton her dress. I tickled her between each button, a ritual which had delighted her since she was very tiny, and she ran off into her room laughing.

A few minutes later when I went in to kiss the girls good night, our eight-year-old was very long-faced and quiet. She looked up.

"Play with *me*, Daddy."

"Oh no," I told her gently, "it's too late, baby."

"You played with sister," she whispered almost weeping.

"No, I didn't, honey, I just unbuttoned her dress."

"But . . . (and now there were tears in her eyes) . . . but, Daddy, I heard her *laughing*."

This morning here in my office I am remembering that little scene, and I realize that although I can outgrow my concern about not being in the mainstream of certain kinds of "parties and games," I will always have the deep need to be included. And this need will drive me out of myself as a solitary Christian and back to God and His people.

··+✦❖✦+··

"Someone has imagined God first fashioning man, and one of the host of heaven, watching, exclaiming in alarm, but you are giving this creature freedom! He will never be wise enough or strong enough to handle it. He will think himself a god. He will boast in his own self-sufficiency. How can you gamble that he will ever return to you? And God replies, I have left him unfinished within. I have left in him deep needs that only I can satisfy, that out of his desire, his homesickness of soul, he will remember to turn to me."[34]

F. B. Speakman
*The Salty Tang*

LORD, thank You that You have called us Christians into a family and not to a lonely way. Thank You that the longing to be included, which seems to be planted in us from the beginning, has finally been met in a relationship with You and Your people. And thank You for the reminder from the past this morning. As I try to witness to that which I have seen and heard of You today, help me to be more aware of other people who come into Your Christian family at church and of their need to *feel* included . . . when they hear laughter across a room, or a city.

"What we have seen and heard we declare to you, so that you and we together may share in a common life, that life which we share with the Father and his Son Jesus Christ. And we write this in order that the joy of us all may be complete."

I John 1:3,4 (NEB)

# Witnessing for the Witness' Sake

THIS MORNING I realized that two very different men had talked to me this week about a common "problem" into which public witnessing has gotten them. One man, named Rick, is very successful materially and has been rather aloof from the average person in his home city for years. Upon making a beginning commitment of his whole life to Christ, he did not like his attitude toward people. But he had not been able to do anything about it.

Being a very talented communicator, Rick was soon asked to speak to groups of laymen concerning his new outlook toward God and people. This past weekend he spoke to 1200 in one meeting. Yesterday he called and laughed, "You crazy fanatics have ruined my whole life style," he said. "Now that so many people know me by sight *as a Christian,* I feel like a 'specimen.' I can't feel easy sneering in traffic snarls anymore. I'm afraid they might be some of the ones who heard me say I'm praying to be more loving. God has finally gotten it across to me through this public speaking, that I really want to be open to people."

The other man, who also made a new beginning with Christ several months ago, is an articulate speaker, too, and has

*117*

been invited to witness concerning his faith in a widening geographical circle. But the problem which has plagued this man has been adultery. He came to God in Christ, "just as he was," helpless. And he felt accepted. But although he had prayed a lot about it, one problem he still had trouble with was an occasional slip with a woman. For some of you this may sound strange, but the man had made a deep commitment to Christ; and it had changed almost every area in his life. He just had a lingering problem with women, about which he had been praying earnestly.

But as he sat across my desk this week, he looked sort of confused. "You know, Keith, this witnessing is answering my own prayers by ruining my outside sex life." He smiled with a slightly guilty look as he continued, "I thought I really wanted to give up other women for God, but I would find myself compulsively going to my old haunts 'just to see' if God had healed me. And I'd get in bed every time. But this week, a couple of days after I witnessed at that big meeting, I got in my car to take a drive. When I got to the bar, a girl came over and said, 'Say, I heard you speak the other night at that big meeting. What you said was great!' " My friend went on to tell me that the girl had assumed he was through with his former adulterous habits. So he responded to her assumption and went home.

Now *I* smiled. "You'd better be careful what you pray for, Joe. The Lord works in strange ways."

He looked at me and grinned like a small boy. "If I keep up this witnessing business, I'm going to have to go a thousand miles from home to find a *chance* to get in trouble." And we both knew he had somehow rounded a corner with his problem.

In thinking about these two men and their experiences, I thought, "They really missed the point. We're supposed to change our behavior because we *want* to in order to align our lives with God's purposes as we can discover them." But I saw how unreal I was being. These men are very intelligent. Both had already known how they wanted to behave for Christ's sake, yet neither had had the motivational strength to break their well-established habit patterns. But in standing up and identifying with Christ and His loving way of living, they each became *acutely conscious* of different ways in which their integrity was being compromised by un-Christian behavior they had previously been able to "set aside" from this central commitment to God. And while this was happening unseen and inside their lives, audiences were marveling at the witness of that which God had already done for them.

Because of this experience, I realized the value, and almost the necessity, of publicly identifying with Christ's way of life in order to trigger the conscious interruption of some conditioned response patterns of a lifetime. Of course, the changes came because their strength was in God as they were trying to follow His way.

But at the same time I knew that if the changes were made only because of "audiences," the new behavior might be merely a shallow Christian conformity which could dissolve with a simple change in environment. The only conscious changes which have lasted in my life have been those I have made because I felt the old behavior really interfered with my relationship to God.

···+‹‹‹›+··

"We become fully conscious only of what we are able to express to someone else. We may already have had a certain inner intuition about it, but it must remain vague so long as it is unformulated."[35]

Paul Tournier
*The Meaning of Persons*

BUT THERE IS A DANGER:

"The eyes of people around us exert a great pressure on our designs. These witnesses force us not to give expression to the evil which arises in the heart; we refrain from evil—and our behavior appears correct. Were it not for them our behavior would look quite different; and it often becomes such as long as we are sure that no other eyes can see us. It happens with some people, that as soon as their outer conditions change and they can live more freely, all that was previously concealed, for fear of being seen by others, bursts out and a formerly well-behaved man becomes a drunkard, a debauchee, or even a robber. All these bad impulses were not born at this moment; they existed before, but were denied expression, whereas now they are given free rein and so become manifest."[36]

Lorenzo Scupoli
*Unseen Warfare*

LORD, thank You that the process of witnessing and writing books about the Life You have made available to us through Christ has helped *me* to remember that I honestly do want to be Your person. I am amazed that I can "forget"; and yet my behavior tells me, again and again, that I have. So Lord, I pray that You will use my attempts at witnessing to teach me if no one else and make me a healthy loving person whose strength is in You.

"Blessed are the men whose strength is in thee, in whose heart are the highways to Zion. . . . They go from strength to strength; the God of gods will be seen in Zion."

Psalm 84:5,7

# The Short Unusual Witness of Bennie Abernathy

THIS MORNING I was thinking of how little we know about communication. I tried to imagine the live television pictures from the moon hitting my brain with pinpoint accuracy after traveling untold thousands of miles through the fantastic speeds of the earth's and moon's orbits and their joint travel around the sun. This kind of communication is more than my father could have even imagined. As a matter of fact, I remember seeing a demonstration with him of the first live television equipment when I was a child. I overheard people saying that it was interesting but would never be feasible, because it could only transmit a stationary picture for a few feet.

Just now I thought about the intimate experience I am having as I communicate with you through this book in your mind, perhaps across thousands of miles . . . conceivably over years of time. And yet, even if I am dead when you read this, my living mind is meeting yours, and we are sharing to some degree the communication I am experiencing as I write. It is eerie, but it is true.

*121*

We may be just beginning to learn about the transmission of information between persons and between God and man. If God is personal in nature and we are to pray, "Our Father . . ." as Christ suggested (Matt. 6:9), then we should expect some sort of response in meaningful terms. It may be that our ability to tune in to God's frequency is blocked by our own self-centered absorption. Perhaps our sin is like "filling our receiving screens with snow." Yet occasionally people get very clear "pictures" of God's answer to a prayer in terms of a meaningful word or image. And whether the contact was actually with God or not, sometimes the depth of the experience carries with it the power to change the life of the person praying, and through him the lives of many others.

Several years ago a good friend named Alan told me about a startling encounter he had just been through. My friend is an intelligent professional man and in some ways a little cynical about things he hears. I certainly do not know if the experience had a transcendent reference, but my friend had been deeply moved by the account he related.

A Christian, an automobile salesman, who was a friend of Alan's, decided he was going to make hospital calls two days each week as a part of his response to Christ's admonition to visit the sick. During a routine telephone call to a man named Bennie Abernathy, with whom he had talked earlier about buying a new car, the salesman, Bert Johnson, reached his potential customer's wife. She said, "Mr. Johnson, I don't think my husband will be needing a new car. He is in the hospital and has incurable cancer. He will probably never get out."

Bert thought to himself, I'll go by to see him, just to say "Hello." When he got to the man's room in the hospital, he had a very superficial conversation. Bennie was nice enough, but Bert didn't know him very well and had no idea how he felt about death. Finally, just before leaving, Bert decided to get in at least a word about the real situation. He turned to the sick man, "Well, I hope the Lord gives you peace about all this," nodding toward his body.

When the man heard Bert, his face lighted with a wonderful smile. "Let me tell you something," he said. "All my life I have never really known what I felt about God. I have heard that a person must 'commit his life to Christ'; or 'be born again'—but I didn't really know how. Yesterday I was lying here very depressed because I did not know what to do to tie my life into God. In desperation I decided to pray. I simply asked God how I could come close to Him." The man's face was very sincere and intense as he remembered the experience. Now he looked into Bert's eyes with great clarity. "And do you know what happened as I prayed? I saw Jesus —here in this room, as real as you are. He was standing over there (he nodded toward the corner), and there were people coming to Him. As they got to where He was, each one would reach inside his own robe and lift out his heart . . . and hand it to Jesus. First there were grown men, all kinds, and then there were the children . . ." Bennie paused as he saw it all again in his mind against the wall in the corner of the room. Bert did not know how long they sat like that, but finally the man looked up calmly and said, "And I gave Him my heart too. He took it, put His other hand on my shoulder and smiled as He said, 'peace.' And then He was gone."

Bert could only nod his head slightly as if in agreement. "That's . . . wonderful," he said softly.

The man in the bed went on thoughtfully, "You know, Mr. Johnson, I realize this whole thing sounds absurd, but it's true. It's the truest thing that ever happened to me. And I am going to tell every person who comes in that door before I die."

And he did.

"... All I can do is indicate indirectly certain events in man's life, which can scarcely be described, which experience spirit as meeting; and in the end, when indirect indication is not enough, there is nothing for me but to appeal, my reader, to the witness of your own mysteries—buried, perhaps, but still attainable."[37]

Martin Buber
*I and Thou*

"A miracle is 'not contrary to nature,' but contrary to what we know as nature."[38]

Augustine
*City of God*

"In the dispute concerning the true God and the truth of religion, there has never happened any miracle on the side of error, and not of truth."[39]

Blaise Pascal
*Pascal's Pensées*

LORD, sometimes in my cynicism I feel as if prayer is autosuggestion and that we are playing games with ourselves when we talk of communicating with You. And then I see the miracles of modern science and realize that we are already experiencing things which point beyond our intellectual horizons to a time when men in this life may be able to communicate mind to mind across thousands of miles. With regard to You, we seem to see through a dim lens now; but I believe with Paul that some day we may communicate face to face. I believe, and I appreciate Your help with my unbelief.

"For our knowledge is imperfect and our prophecy is imperfect; but when the perfect comes, the imperfect will pass away. When I was a child, I spoke like a child,

I thought like a child, I reasoned like a child; when I became a man, I gave up childish ways. For now we see in a mirror dimly, but then face to face. Now I know in part; then I shall understand fully, even as I have been fully understood."

I Corinthians 13:9–12

# A New Threshold

HURRAH! through several years of struggling to learn to live for God, I have been tiptoeing in a certain area. I have been very quiet about being a Christian when I am around atheistic philosophers and academic psychologists. I have let the humanism and scientism of some bright but ordinary minds intimidate me. But that is no longer the case. Recently I have realized that the assertion, "God *is*," is *at least* as philosophically sound as the belief that He is not. And after many years of checking this hypothesis as it is developed in the Christian gospel, I am persuaded that Christianity makes considerably more sense than atheism.

In struggling for my own handle by which to grasp the Christian faith with integrity, something profound has happened to me. As I was wrestling with the intellectual problems of believing, I was also learning to live a life in which I prayed, studied devotionally, and talked to other people about Christ. One day recently I was thinking about the gospel and logic when I realized that along the way somewhere I have become hopelessly in love with God. I have seen that experience comes alive and glows with light for me only as it revolves around His life and purposes as these are

*126*

revealed in Christ and His people. I am suddenly and wonderfully not ashamed of my identification with the church.

How presumptuous and simple this must sound to anyone who has never ached and wept with frustration and disappointment over the church and the nature of its life, or lack of life, in the world. For years I have been free and proud to be a Christian in lay groups and at congregational meetings. But to be identified with the church in the academic world was a very difficult step. I have seen and been a part of so much of the sickness and soft thinking of the church that I have avoided this open identification for years—for fear I would lose forever the possibility of the respect of thinking men.

But now Christianity is coming into an historical perspective. I understand in a deeper way that the solutions to a divided world's problems politically and economically depend on a common acceptance of some Person or Purpose beyond any country's individual interests. I see God as the unifying hope for peace and international cooperation, really for the first time. I had read this notion years ago in Plato's Republic and heard it in sermons. But now I can grasp it at the depth of my being. Even as I write this, I am aware that such an abstract idea is politically naïve at this time. But I think that one day it will not be naïve at all.

I guess my own experience has taught me that the profound solution to the deepest human problems must wait until we have tried the more superficial answers involving our own clever manipulations. Then, when we see that outwitting our opponents does not win their love or loyalty and bring peace —then in our desperation, we may look into such "abstractions" as faith. And we may find that the truth of Christianity has in some strange way become personal, real, and very practical.

". . . if many modern philosophers and men of science could have had their way, they would have been dissuading Greeks, Jews, and Mohammedans from such useless studies [as mathematics], from such pure abstractions for which no foresight could divine the ghost of an application. Luckily they could not get at their ancestors."[40]

Alfred North Whitehead
*The Adventure of Ideas*

WITH REGARD TO PROOF OF GOD:

"Perhaps the only thing that anyone can be absolutely sure of is that he will never be able to prove it either way —with objective, verifiable proof. We can know that in the beginning there was God and not just some cosmic upheaval that brought light out of darkness only when we have experienced him doing the same thing in our lives, our world—bringing light out of our darkness.

"To put it another way, unless there is some very real sense in which the Spirit of God moves over the dark and chaotic waters of this age, these deeps of yours and mine; unless God speaks his light and life giving word to me, then I do not really care much one way or the other whether he set the whole show spinning x billion of years ago."[41]

Frederick Buechner
*The Magnificent Defeat*

LORD, thank You for the joy of discovery and for occasionally allowing us to break through the fences of smaller mental pastures into larger ones through faith. Help me to begin looking at history, government, and economics as You see them—rather than seeing only the personal issues of life. Help me never to be ashamed of You or Your message which is transforming my own experience of life. Give me a new dimension of freedom and courage to witness for You. This is a frightening threshold, Lord. The future is uncertain. Please give me Your hand.

··+❧❦❧+··

"For I am not ashamed of the gospel: it is the power of God for salvation to every one who has faith, to the Jew first and also to the Greek."

Romans 1:16

"For God has allowed us to know the secret of his plan, and it is this: he purposes in his sovereign will that all human history shall be consummated in Christ, that every thing that exists in Heaven or earth shall find its perfection and fulfillment in him."

Ephesians 1:9,10 (Phillips)

# The Hinge Is Small

THE LONGER I am involved in the Christian life, the more clearly I see that the beginnings of significant life-long changes often hinge on seemingly insignificant discoveries and decisions in the intimate arena of personal relationships.

Some time ago about twelve of us got together to form a small group. We were trying to find out how we could learn to be God's people away from the church during the week. This was a new adventure which was exciting for most of the group. We decided that we would not tell anyone else what we were doing. The idea was to attempt various experiments in our lives during the week and then report to the group what happened to us.

Our plan was to begin in our families and work outward into the world. During the first week we were to look around, listen in our homes and see what *we* were doing to bug the people we live with, and then pray about our behavior to see if we could change it. Usually in prayer groups we had looked for those things other people were doing to bother us and then prayed for *them* to change. This is a very different approach.

The next week was an interesting one. One member of our group was a lovely, pleasingly plump, white-haired lady who

**130**

was very attractive. At the first meeting I remember thinking that Lillian looked almost angelic . . . with a slight twinkle in her eye. She didn't seem to have any problems and prayed sweet, sincere prayers. Frankly, I wondered how she got in our group. Lillian had not said much so far, but she came into the next meeting like a rodeo rider out of chute four. She was so excited she was practically bubbling over. When I asked the group about the experiment, all Lillian could say was, "You all, it's the *shirts!*"

All I could think of to say was, "Would you like to talk about it?"

She went on, "I'm from the old South. And when I got married, my mother told me, 'Don't you ever iron any man's shirts. That's not wives' work.' So after the honeymoon twenty-five years ago, I told my husband I was not going to iron his shirts. He was a struggling student at that time, and we didn't have very much money, but he had to send his shirts out. After a few years, he developed a rash on his neck and had to wear shirts which required hand ironing. So for sixteen years Bill has been getting up on Saturday mornings and ironing his own shirts—right in front of me while I fixed breakfast. We were both Christians, but about that time we started going to different churches."

She stopped talking and put her fist against her mouth, and her bosom shook with an involuntary sob. In a moment she went on with tears in her eyes: "This week I discovered that all my guilt and self-hate as a woman, all of the wrangling and separation I've caused in our marriage, stems from the fact that I wouldn't iron Bill's shirts. I've prayed all week, and I don't know if I can do anything this late to change things for Bill . . . but I'd like for you to pray for me that I will." And we did.

Well, I don't know what Lillian did at home those next few

days, but the following week Bill showed up at the meeting, smiling from ear to ear. And they came to the group together regularly like two happy kids until Lillian died suddenly of a stroke a year later. But you know, that couple found each other, found a new kind of life together after twenty-five years.

What is that experience worth in terms of changing the world? I don't know, but watching it happen changed the rest of us in that group somehow. We began to see that the closed doors in our lives and relationships which we have been trying to batter down with argument and reason all these years—that those doors often swing open on small rusty hinges, on little things . . . like the shirts.

··+◄◄⊰║⊱►►·+··

"Indeed, this need of individuals to be right is so great that they are willing to sacrifice themselves, their relationships, and even love for it. This need to be right is also one which produces hostility and cruelty, and causes people to say things that shut them off from communication with both God and man."[42]

Ruel Howe
*The Miracle of Dialogue*

··+◄◄⊰║⊱►►·+··

LORD, help me to have the courage to look for the little inner walls and fortresses in my relationships, behind which I protect my pride. Forgive me for camouflaging these defenses and calling them "matters of principle" when so often they are only means to keep from having to admit that I have been wrong and wanted to be number one. I guess this is what has always made You so threatening to me. When You expose my self-justifying defenses, I either have to confess them or put You down . . . which is what I guess we tried to do on the Cross. And I still try to put You down when you get close to revealing the motives I have hidden. Help me, Lord, not to cling to my "rights" but to unclench my spiritual fist so that I can be free to follow You.

·•✦❉✦•·

"Let Christ Jesus be your example as to what your attitude should be. For he, who had always been God by nature, did not cling to his prerogatives as God's equal, but stripped himself of all privilege by consenting to be a slave . . . and . . . he humbled himself by living a life of utter obedience, even to the extent of dying . . ."

Philippians 2:5–8 (Phillips)

# A Christian Father: The Artful Dodger

O NE OF THE most subtle problems I have found as a "committed and active" Christian is this: those of us who begin to minister to others sometimes start to take on a sort of Holy Immunity from some of the normal responsibilities of family life, because of our "high calling." For instance, any normal husband would catch hell if he were gone from home in the evenings half as much as the average minister is. Although it is true that I have often been as upset as my wife about having to be away from our family so much, it is also true that when the children were small, there was often a great relief in bypassing the thousands of details and questions with which our little girls plagued us in that rather frantic twilight period near the end of the day. And often when I was at home physically, I was absent emotionally.

Because of the lack of dependability of my presence with the girls when they were still quite young, Mary Allen was forced to assume the underlying responsibility for their growth and development. But the thing about this responsibility that seems to be particularly frustrating to wives is that it is only felt by the one who accepts it. So I did not even realize that there was such a burden, much less that I was not bearing my part of it. My ignorance of this problem led to no small amount of resentment in Mary Allen's life. She felt that to bring up my continual absence "for the Lord's work" would make her look like a lazy or nagging wife and a poor Christian. When she would bring it up, her tone was so loaded with resentment that I sort of felt she was those things.

But at a pastors and wives conference recently I counseled with a number of women, most of whom were married to prominent ministers. Several of them felt emotionally deserted with their children. And the husband, if confronted, had been irritated that the wife couldn't "do her part." Or he had retreated behind the ministerial shield with the guilt-provoking insinuation that however much he wishes it were different, "The Lord's work must come first." Some have even referred to the passage where Jesus' family came to get Him while he was speaking to a group, and He refused to come out (Mk. 3:31).

But as I began to see that these women were genuinely hurt, bewildered, and felt terribly alone with the emotional responsibility for their children, I started looking into it—especially since it seemed to be so common. That was when it occurred to me that *I* was doing the same thing to my own family.

Later, at home, I reread Mark 3:31 and discovered one thing immediately that would blast a legalist: When Jesus would not leave the group to whom He was ministering to go out to His family, He was talking about His *parental* family (mother and siblings). But He was not talking about leaving His wife and children in order to stay with the group to whom he was preaching.

I realize this may sound like scriptural nit-picking, but there is a great deal of difference in the responsibility for the marital family one instigates and the parental family he is *supposed* to leave. For in other places the Scriptures say that a man is to give second place to his parental family and give his *first* attention to the family represented by his marriage (Gen. 2:24, Eph. 5:31). And of course the New Testament Epistles are pretty clear about a Christian (particularly an ordained minister) bearing his responsibilities to his wife and children (Eph. 5:25, I Pet. 3:7, I Tim. 3:4, 12, 3:12 and Tit. 1:6).

If this were true, I had a reorientation job on my hands . . . with my own life. I began to realize that my unconscious avoiding of a good bit of the constant nitty-gritty of family living had made me hesitant to preach or teach about intimate life in the home. And yet so much of the distress of new Christians seemed to center in bruised family relations, but how could I speak about problems I *still had?* So what I often did was to avoid this issue and talk about "more important matters" . . . like prayer or social involvement. And this way I avoided facing the true nature of my holy immunity.

But as I continued to read about the life, death, and resurrection of Jesus Christ, I saw One who refused to witness or preach from a favored position. Although He was probably never married, He lived and witnessed out of an authentic life in which He was as vulnerable as the people to whom He ministered. I began to see that unless I can try to be a genuine, participating father and husband, sharing the emotional responsibilities for my family's growth and happiness, I have nothing to say about an authentic life in Christ to the families around us.

How do I find a balance in all this? For I must be away from home more than some men. And yet I must find a way to include every member of my family in the shifting circle of my inner emotional horizon. How do I build each one of them into a calendar already filled with important and even necessary dates? I do not know how I can, but only that I must. (Tomorrow I will talk about some things I have tried.)

·+·✦✧✦·+·

"The 'great' commitment all too easily obscures the 'little' one. But without the humility and warmth which you have to develop in your relations to the few with whom you are personally involved, you will never be able to do anything for the many. Without them, you will live in a world of abstractions, where your solipsism, your greed for power, and your death wish lack the one opponent which is stronger than they—love."⁴³

Dag Hammarskjold
*Markings*

·+·✦✧✦·+·

LORD, help me not to take myself and my work so seriously that I fail to be a husband and father to those special people You have given to me alone, to love and care for in Your name. If I fail with my mission as a witness to the community, You can raise others; but if I fail as a father to provide for the needs of those in my own home, there are no others to fill the void. This frightens me, Lord, because I don't know how to be a good husband and father, and I have let my own dreams and resentments keep me from facing my inadequacies. Help me to begin to learn how to be genuine and unselfishly loving in my own home.

·+·✦✧✦·+·

"If any one does not provide for his relatives, and especially for his own family, he has disowned the faith and is worse than an unbeliever."

I Timothy 5:8

# An Injection for the Calendar

YESTERDAY, after I wrote about the problems of being a husband and father when one's calendar is loaded with trips and meetings, I jotted down some things which have been helpful to me in trying to move from the periphery toward the mainstream of our family's on-going life.

When I first started praying about trying to be a better father and husband, I made some disconcerting discoveries. In the first place I am controlled by habit to a larger extent than I realized. In certain ways I had put "other people" and "my ministry" (or business ventures) ahead of my family for so long, that I did not know how to begin changing without going overboard in the other direction.

These are some of the mechanical changes I made to get back into the bloodstream of our family's life: At the first of each year, I take my new appointment calendar and write on each family member's birthday, "Commitment to family." Then I do the same thing with our wedding anniversary, and I try to plan a vacation time with the family and put it on the calendar. For a while I added a couple of random two-day "commitments" so that Mary Allen and I could get away together. Later in the year, when some new project came up or someone called about a meeting which fell on one of the

*138*

family's days, I said without any hesitation, "I'm sorry but I already have a commitment on that date."

I remember the first time an invitation to participate in a big meeting came on one of the children's birthdays. I was very interested in the meeting but said "no." The man, who was a friend, must have sensed my hesitation, because he asked, "Why can't you come? This is an important convention and your witness might reach a lot of people."

I was a little embarrassed to say that it was "my little girl's birthday," but I went on to tell him, "You can get half a dozen speakers in an hour, but I am the only daddy she's got."

He was quiet on the other end of the line for a few seconds, and I thought he had rejected me as a fool. Then he said quietly, "I wish I could do that." And I knew I had started in the right direction.

Before that time, I had been away on three family birthdays in a row. Now, I hardly ever miss a birthday unless something comes up that seems to warrant a very special exception, and we can all agree to slide the celebration to another date.

Another thing which has helped Mary Allen and me is to try to get a sitter and go out of town for a day or two by ourselves. We generally go to a nearby city to avoid the expenditure of time, money, and energy required for a long trip. We check in a hotel and relax. We may window-shop, read, see movies, eat quiet meals together, sleep late, and not even contact people we know well. These mini-vacations without the children help each of us know that we are being heard by the other and do something special for our relationship. I realize that many people cannot afford the money for this kind of "taking off." But we have gone when we could not afford it, and somehow the sacrifice has said to us that our relationship is very important. But if traveling is out, a little creative thought may help a couple to come up with another way to find time alone away from the children.

As to specific ways one relates to his wife and children at home, that which is natural for one man will not be for another. But the thing good fathers and husbands seem to have in common is the ability to make each member of the family feel important, and that old dad is "aware" of their needs and their accomplishments. The message I am trying to get across to my family is: "Although I am a busy person who will probably always be away from home some, each of you is very important to me. Among people, you are *first* in my life."

There have been times when this was impossible to say, because I was mad, or anxious, or because I was off trying to participate in the building of a new kingdom for God (or for me). But I try to come back again and again and build time for my family into the fabric of my life. I do this because I love them. And I have to resort to mechanical means because it is so easy for me to avoid the responsibility of thinking of anyone but me.

I may not make as many speeches, attend as many meetings, or write as many books for Christ. But I hope I will at least have lived for Him in my own home.

···

"For the trouble is that we are self-centred, and no effort of the self can remove the self from the centre of its own endeavour; the very effort will plant it there the more fixedly than ever. The man of science is drawn out of himself as regards one whole range of his activity by the concentration of his attention on the object of his study in his search for truth; the artist, by a similar concentration in his search for beauty; the good man, or public-spirited man, by a similar concentration in the service of his cause. But none of these cover the whole of life. Always there remains a self-centred area of life, and sometimes by a natural process of compensation those who are most selfless in the search for truth or beauty, or in public service, are most selfish, fretful and querulous at home."[44]

William Temple
*Nature, Man and God*

··+·❄❖❄·+··

LORD, You know how many days I cannot turn loose and be a good husband, how many times my mind is filled with visions of my work or myself. Yet I want to be Your person in our home. I love my family very much. But sometimes my behavior tells me I love what I am doing more. Help me to find a balance, so I can be free in my work and yet enjoy being the person my family needs.

··+·❄❖❄·+··

"Enjoy life with the wife whom you love, all the days of your vain life which he has given you under the sun, because that is your portion in life and in your toil at which you toil under the sun."

Ecclesiastes 9:9

# An Earthen Vessel

THIS MORNING I am lonely. Mary Allen and the children are here, and we love each other very much. But I am facing some fears of failure which cannot be shared with them. I feel that my performance on a very important examination involving the future for all of us will not be adequate, and I'm anxious and afraid, like a small boy. Yet God seems very near. If I fail, He will be there, and I can pick up whatever pieces there are and do something else. And this gives me a deep underlying courage. But the conditioned franticness which makes my mind a beehive of fears is a carry-over from a lifetime of feeling that I must succeed to be acceptable.

This paradox is hard to understand—a sincere commitment to Christ combined with human insecurity in the face of failure. And many of the great Christian speakers and writers have left me alone in my predicament by neglecting to tell me of these paradoxes of the inner journey. As I have read devotional books and listened to the evangelists and teachers of the faith, I have tried to reconstruct from their words a picture of the inner way. But they have omitted so much of the sweat and gravel from their descriptions of the Christian life that I am left with visions of untroubled saints, walking

through the quiet sterile corridors of their souls with un-
changing attitudes of serenity and courage.

But I am finding that serenity and courage are very different in "appearance" from inside my own life. And as I
counsel with other Christians, I realize that I am not alone in
this. The record of Dietrich Bonhoeffer, as he wrote from the
Nazi prison camp before his martyr's death, sounds stimulating and rather glorious at first glance. But as I read his
letters* more closely, the actual daily experience *for Bonhoeffer* seems to have been very different. Much of it was
made up of the buzzing whine of summer flies around his
face, the maddening frustration and disappointment as his
hopes for release were agonizingly prolonged or smashed,
fear and doubts, and despair. All of these were things which
often filled his mind as he lived out those days and nights of
"marvelous Christian discipline and courage." Yet because
of the paradoxical joy and hope he experienced, Bonhoeffer
was able to go through that miserable imprisonment and
make of it a great positive sign for all of Christendom. And
this same paradox faces thousands of ordinary men and
women who are trapped in jobs or marriages which seem
impossible. But because they think that a "truly committed
Christian" should *feel* victorious, they hide their painful
loneliness and the guilt it brings.

This morning as I am confronted by the threat of changing
to a new vocational direction in midstream of life with my
bridges burned behind me, I *can* risk it because of my faith in
Christ. But the fear of failure rides with me in the pit of my
stomach as I go to the examination which determines the next
chapter in our lives.

---

* Bonhoeffer, Dietrich, *Prisoner for God: Letters and Papers from
Prison* (New York: The Macmillan Company, 1961).

If I pass the test and "succeed" in my new venture, some of my friends may say some day, "What courage, to have launched out in faith at your age!" And I wonder if I will remember the anxiety that makes my palms sweat as I write this. Or will I only smile, "give God the credit " humbly, and forget to tell how slender the thread of faith seems which I am following through the jungle of my fears right now?

·+◄◙▒►+·

"I have repeatedly observed here how few there are who can make room for conflicting emotions at the same time. When the bombers come, they are all fear; when there is something good to eat, they are all greed . . . By contrast, Christianity plunges us into many different dimensions of life simultaneously."[45]

Dietrich Bonhoeffer
*Prisoner for God*


"It is rather in *overt* behavior that we must look for a measure of belief, and it is principally this that is inhibited in doubt or disbelief."[46]

D. E. Berlyne

·+◄◙▒►+·

LORD, thank You that You give us the courage to go ahead and "risk it" occasionally in trying to follow You, forgiveness when we "chicken out" and cannot, and the clean slate of a new day after each of our failures and denials. In my attempts to witness to the hope and joy of Your presence in ordinary life, help me not to whitewash the frailty of the humanity into which it came to dwell as I try to trust You in everything. I am grateful that even You had some struggles in facing the challenges in Your life.

·+◄◙▒►+·

"Anguish and dismay came over him, and . . . He went on a little, fell on his face in prayer, and said, 'My

Father, if it is possible, let this cup pass me by. Yet not
as I will, but as thou wilt.' "

Jesus Christ
Matthew 26:38, 39 (NEB)

# A New World in the Midst
# of the Old One

A FUNNY THING happened this week. Our daughter Kristin, who is 15 years old, has been learning to drive. She is a very alert girl and is always aware of where we are and where we are going when we are out driving as a family. I am not. I often drive for blocks past a turn-off with my mind a thousand miles away. But Kristin is the one who often sits beside me and whispers, "This next block is our turn, Daddy." She knows our town with her eyes closed.

But this week when she got behind the wheel for the first time in traffic, it was as if we were in a new city: "Do I turn here, Daddy? . . . Is this the right street?"

I was amazed and thought at first that she was teasing me. But then I saw that she was not. A town that she had known like the back of her hand as a passenger became a strange and foreign place when she became responsible for the minute-by-minute decisions of driving. She had to look for a whole new set of objects and distances. She had to see cars backing out of driveways, puppy dogs and children starting for the street, vehicles at intersections, all kinds of street signs, in addition to everything behind her in the rear view mirror. With all of these new things on which to focus in the foreground of her attention—which had heretofore been only a part of the background—she felt as if she were in a different world.

I started to fuss at her and tell her to "pay attention to what you are doing!" Then I realized that she was very serious and *was* paying attention. But she was experiencing a reorientation in the same situation because of trying to focus on different elements of her environment. So I said nothing and kept telling myself it was the end result of her training which was important.

As we drove along, I began to understand why it may be that newly committed Christians appear to be sort of "out of it." For a while, they seem to be like Kristin behind the wheel —in a kind of daze in which the world they have known appears to be totally different. Because of accepting the responsibility of a new relationship with God and focusing on loving Him and His people, they seem to be unaware of things and people to whom they once paid attention quite naturally. Many ministers or relatives are hurt and surprised when a church member gets "turned on" at some sort of lay renewal meeting and begins paying less attention to them because of his new Christian friends. They suspect that the new commitment was to a cult of some sort of self-centered pietists. The temptation is to be very judgmental of people experiencing this reorientation.

I do not know how one really ought to handle this situation. But by the end of the week (in our car) I noticed that Kristin knew where she was again. And now she can include both the old things she used to see . . . and the new things she needed to see to grow up and get on down the road.

···

"When we treat man as he is, we make him worse than he is. When we treat him as if he already were what he potentially could be, we make him what he should be."[47]

Goethe

"In training a horse, it is important not to break his spirit because it is his spirit, during and after the training period, which will determine his style and endurance. Does education, we may ask, allow for the expression of the wildness of vitality during the educational process, or does it repress vitality in the interest of form and conformity?"[48]

Reuel Howe
*The Miracle of Dialogue*

"A . . . peculiarity of the assurance state is the objective change which the world often appears to undergo. 'An appearance of newness beautifies every object.' "[49]

William James
*Varieties of Religious Experience*

LORD, help us to be patient with new Christians who seem to have lost their perspective as they have entered a new relationship with You. If they become temporarily blinded to the ordinary responsibilities and the old friends around them, help us to provide an atmosphere in which this new relationship with You can be tested and translated into deeper relationships with people. Help us in the church to let new Christians enjoy the excitment of discovery without our hypercritical judgment—even though there may be some anxious moments about their soundness and responsibility.

"And all were amazed and perplexed, saying to one another, 'What does this mean?' But others mocking said, 'They are filled with new wine.' "

Acts 2:12,13

"Therefore, if any one is in Christ, he is a new creation; the old has passed away, behold, the new has come."

II Corinthians 5:17

# The Hardening of the Heart

THIS WEEK my prayers are filled with thoughts and plans of what I am going to do. I have been considering a new business venture. My mind is going over the proposal like a spider crawling around a baseball looking for a crack, a place to get inside the problems the business is supposed to solve. I am trying to determine whether a corporation or joint venture would be best for everyone involved. Since I was first attracted to the enterprise because it represented a possible solution to a problem in the church, I began with visions of how I would be doing God's work in the business. But more and more, the excitement centers around ways I could make a lot of money out of the deal.

I know that thinking about the profit potential is absolutely necessary before a business can be established. And I realize that a prayer time might be the best circumstance in which to consider a new business venture. But I have been disturbed by the course my own thoughts have taken about everything this week when I have prayed each morning. I have found myself becoming a calculating person, shrewdly assessing the day's activities and relationships in terms of financial criteria. Although it is very subtle, I have looked at the world as an orchard to be picked by me and for me and my family. The tricky part about what happened at this point is that other people did not seem to notice any change . . . at first. My outward responses were still basically positive toward people. But inside I developed a cool, detached feeling about them and found my thoughts were more manipulative than loving.

As the cycle continued its course, my family began to complain that I was grouchy, and they seemed to become a little "distant." I became terribly busy and started to feel somewhat isolated and empty. I finally woke up to the fact that my prayers were dry, that I was skipping them pretty regularly, and that I was beginning to be miserable inside. My heart felt cold toward God.

Today I have seen that this hardening process begins when I start getting grandiose visions of building great enterprises in which I am the center. And I recalled that this process has happened before. The road back to Christ is a hard one for me, because I cannot seem to realize the progressive way such thinking makes me preoccupied and causes me to stride roughshod over the feelings of those around me. I am like a tethered elephant stepping on his own brood.

But finally the "cold drafts" around the house and my own sense of busy isolation from God break through into my attention. And I realize that I have drifted away from being personal with Christ and with my family. At last, I have to confess that I have tried again to be "the King," to be God in my own little world . . . and that like a little boy with his candy, too much projected glory has made me spiritually sick at my stomach. I see that instead of following Christ, I have jogged ahead and tried to point out to Him the way we are to go.

I have subtly slipped the keys to my future out of His pocket and dropped them in mine. And I have to dig deeply and fork them over, telling Him that I really want to be His person and to participate in the doing of His will, instead of trying to be a Big Cheese in His world. Or if I cannot honestly tell Him that I *want* to do this, then I tell Him that I would like to want to.

When I can truly turn to Christ again in this way, a remarkable thing happens. I leave my time of prayer more open to those around me, less hard and more gentle. Somehow on such days I feel more at home in the world. And when I am dealing with people, I find myself seeking our mutual advantage in business instead of only mine. But I know I must stay close to Him with a daily surrender or I will be off again on my own. And it may take weeks for me to find out that I have picked the Lord's pocket and am galloping off over the cobblestones of my family's hearts with my future in my fist.

·•◄╬╣►•·

"Some there are that resign themselves, but with certain reservations, and put not their full trust in God; therefore they consider how best to provide for themselves. Some also at first offer all; but afterwards, having succumbed to temptation, they revert to their former state and make no progress in the path of virtue. These will obtain neither true freedom of heart nor the grace of My gracious friendship, unless with complete resignation, they offer themselves as a daily oblation unto Me. Without this surrender, there neither is, nor can be, any lasting and fruitful union with Me."[50]

Thomas à Kempis
*The Imitation of Christ*

". . . without thee all health is but the fuel, and all strength but the bellows of sin."[51]

John Donne
*Private Devotions*

·•◄╬╣►•·

THANK YOU, GOD, that You win our hearts not once, but again and again. I am grateful that You did not reject the disciples when they wanted to be the greatest. And thank You for the hope and confidence that You not only receive us prodigals back into your presence, but that You even put us to work in your vineyard again.

·⊷◆⊰⊱◆⊶·

"No servant can be the slave of two masters; for either he will hate the first and love the second, or he will be devoted to the first and think nothing of the second. You cannot serve God and Money. . . ."

Jesus Christ
Luke 16:13 (NEB)

# The Lack of Tangible
# Results—a Problem

THIS IS ONE of those days when I am confused about Christianity. I believe; I am glad that I am a Christian— and yet nothing seems to happen of a lasting nature as a result of my witnessing for Christ. Knowing that this is a self-centered attitude doesn't seem to help much either.

In thinking about this problem of "results" just now, I remembered an early morning meeting yesterday with some men about whom I care a great deal. Charles Sumners, the minister of a large church in our city for more than thirty years, was speaking: "Sometimes I get discouraged. I can't see that my work with people is really changing anything. And as for my own belief in God, in a life after death, in the basic tenets of the faith—in the last analysis I am right where I was at the beginning of my ministry—I can only trust and hope that these things are true. Although I can see that realis- tically the church has grown and prospered in terms of mem- bers and material things, I cannot see that much has hap- pened spiritually because of my ministry here."

No one said a word. We all love and respect this man a great deal, and he was baring his heart to us. As I sat in the

**153**

silence, a picture passed through my mind. It was Sunday and
Charles was standing in the pulpit. He was still quite weak
after spending several days in the hospital and it was obvious
to me that he was struggling with his sermon. But at the
conclusion he told us that during his sickness he had seen
once more the basic message of his ministry—that God loves
us and has amazingly given us the gift of life in Christ. He
became very enthusiastic and alive; it was as if he had just
discovered this idea. I was afraid he might get too emotional,
because of his weakened condition, and overtire himself. But
at that point Charles stopped, looked at us with great calm,
and concluded simply, "And I have found again in my own
experience that I believe in Jesus Christ, and this belief is
transforming my life."

Having finished his sermon, he sat down, probably discouraged again at our seeming lack of response. And yet my heart
was singing. Somehow as he had said those words, filtered
through a life which fairly radiated with courage and openness, I believed again too, and was excited with the renewed
freshness of this discovery.

Then a young man in the prayer group yesterday morning
responded to the minister's confession in an affirming way.
And although the older man was grateful for the affirmation,
it seemed to me he really could not accept it as true.

Since he was leaving town for a few days of rest, Charles
excused himself from our group before the closing prayers.
After he left, someone said thoughtfully, almost in amaze-
ment, "You know, he has *no idea* what the witness of his life
has meant to those of us in his church." In the silence that
followed a well-respected minister of another church said
quietly . . . "In this whole *city*." In the closing prayers he
poured out his gratitude for the strengthening influence of
Charles Sumners in his own life and work. But of course

Charles did not hear the depth of gratitude the man expressed.

As the meeting broke up, it came to me: none of us can see with much accuracy the results of his own efforts, because so much of a Christian's influence has to do with the depth of his own personal inner life. To the Christian himself it seems like a battleground of losses and retreats, marred with old scars and shell holes. But from the *outside,* other people may see only the aura of love and concern which seem to surround those who commit themselves wholly to the finding and doing of God's will and the loving of His people.

I realize now that most of us will never be able to know accurately the long-term effects of anything we try to do. But it doesn't matter so much, because I can see that the kind of spiritual influence which appears to have deep roots and lasting affects is not usually projected consciously. Such influence seems to be a by-product of a style of living. People are evidently touched unconsciously through the Christian's eyes and hands as he tries to help them, and as he points beyond himself . . . to tell them about Christ and His healing love.

·+·◄◊►·+·

"Even coherence with God's perfect will leaves reason in restless clash with the actual. Thus while faith can free reason from basic anxiety it can never rest it in any complacent solution."[52]

Nels Ferré
*Faith and Reason*

·+·◄◊►·+·

DEAR GOD, I am very grateful that You left us the stories— like "the widow's mite"—about the importance to You of the efforts and gifts of ordinary people who have no great credentials in terms of fame and material statistics. Help me to remember that You do not judge as we do. And thank You that even as You give us peace, You give us a restlessness which moves us always beyond ourselves to seek and love other people. Thank You that You make me want to do great things for You, but thank You even more that Your love is not contingent on my getting them done.

⋅⋅✦✥⋗◈⋖✥✦⋅⋅

"Therefore, my beloved brethren, be steadfast, immovable, always abounding in the work of the Lord, knowing that in the Lord your labor is not in vain."

I Corinthians 15:58

# Prayer: A Wisdom of Its Own

D O YOU BELIEVE that God is omniscient—that He knows all that we are thinking?" he asked me. I said that I did. The young man smiled with a little condescension as he sprang his logical trap, which was calculated to discredit the whole idea of prayer.

"Well, then," he continued, "if *He* already knows I have committed a particular sin and *I* already know it, doesn't it seem a little childish for me to tell *Him what He already knows*? Therefore, I see no logical reason for a Christian to confess anything to God."

I was with a sharp group of college students late one night at a leadership conference. The other Christian kids in the group seemed very interested in the boy's logic. I just felt tired. As I thought about his question, my mind went back to a marital counseling situation several years before and to something I had read fifteen years earlier by Randolph Crump Miller.*

"Let me set up a situation for you," I said. I asked the boy if he were married. He was. "Let's say you went home from this conference a day early," I continued, "and as you were

---

* Miller, Randolph Crump, *The Clue to Christian Education.*

going in your house you happened to notice the light on in the bedroom next door. Through the window you saw your wife in the act of committing adultery. Later she came home and said nothing about the affair with the neighbor. Now *you* already know she has sinned against your marriage, and *she* already knows it. But is there any real chance for a trusting, open relationship between you in the future unless she confesses to you *that which you both already know?*"

I watched the boy grasp the truth I had read years earlier and saw him shake his head at the apparent paradox of confession and restoration. I realized that he had been thinking about Christianity as another logical philosophical system, and that I think of it as a loving, family type relationship with God and with people. In our marriage Mary Allen and I have discovered that the dynamics of healthy intimate relations for us are ruled by a kind of personal wisdom and concern that transcend formal logic, and often seem to contradict it. Yet *within* such a good marriage, for instance, the rules and energy governing love, hate, failure, confession, forgiveness, and restoration have a profound and compelling kind of logic of their own, which those outside such a relationship can never grasp at a personal level.

As I drove home from the meeting that night I could remember a good many marriages, and even business partnerships, which had gone on the rocks—when "logic and justice" were substituted for the healing power of confession and forgiveness—even though all the parties already knew the *facts* about the broken relationship involved.

·+·◄◊►·+·

"We are like earthworms, cabbages, and nebulae, objects of divine knowledge. But when we . . . assent with all our wills to be so known, then we treat ourselves, in relation to God, not as things but as persons. We have

unveiled. Not that any veil could have baffled this sight.
The change is in us. The passive changes to the active.
Instead of merely being known, we show, we tell, we
offer ourselves to view."[53]

C. S. Lewis
"Episcopalian"

"Through prayer, religion insists, things which cannot
be realized in any other manner come about: energy
which but for prayer would be bound is by prayer set
free and operates in some part, be it objective or subjec-
tive, of the world of facts."[54]

William James
*The Varieties of Religious Experience*

LORD, thank You for the wisdom, the pattern, and the power
of the continually reconciling relationship which you designed and revealed through the life, death, and resurrection
of Jesus Christ. Help me to come to You and to tell You what
I know about my sin; and then give me a new heart to love
with today. When I am proud and want to bypass confession,
then break my heart rather than let me only bow in Your
direction and turn from You in my daily living. Stay with me,
Lord, so I can stay with You.

"Create in me a clean heart, O God, and put a new and
right spirit within me. Cast me not away from thy presence, and take not thy holy Spirit from me. . . . O Lord,
open thou my lips, and my mouth shall show forth thy
praise. For thou hast no delight in sacrifice; were I to
give a burnt offering, thou wouldst not be pleased. The
sacrifice acceptable to God is a broken spirit; a broken
and contrite heart, O God, thou wilt not despise."

Psalm 51:10,11; 15–17

# Resenting the People—A Minister's Trap . . . with Room for All

G OOD MORNING!" he said—too brightly, it seemed to me— "Did you get a good night's sleep?"

I just looked at him for a few seconds as he walked past me into my motel room. *He had to be kidding.* This man had brought me back to the motel after midnight from the meeting with college kids, *after* the reception, *after* the big meeting in the church's sanctuary . . . which had come *on the heels* of a small dinner party. I had arrived in town about five o'clock from an all day flight, following some similar marathon-type-church meetings the week before. Now at 6:30 the same morning he was picking me up to take me to an "informal breakfast" with about a hundred men to whom I was to speak. I was so tired that I felt a little sick at my stomach.

Actually, I liked the man who was standing there talking to me. He is a great guy and I think he is honest, courageous, and a deeply committed Christian minister. But something was definitely wrong between us. Then I recognized my feelings—resentment, raw resentment, and I had not even been able to admit it consciously. I was mad at myself, too, for letting him get me into all this. I recalled telling him over

*160*

the telephone that I was very tired and had three strenuous days of meetings immediately following my "stop off" with him. So he had originally planned a gathering for me to get acquainted with a few of the people who had been involved in small groups in his church. But the real purpose of my stopping, as I had understood it, was so that the minister and I could get acquainted.

The intimate dinner party was pleasant, but there was a large crowd at the evening meeting. Then after I spoke, there were thirty minutes of direct questions—followed by two later "unscheduled" meetings. To have refused to speak again would have seemed un-Christian, even though I was exhausted. I guess I had expected him to "protect me" or say "no" for me, but since he did not, I was resentful and was mad at myself too. Why was I angry, though? Everything had gone well, and I am committed to witnessing, to giving my life to Christ and His people. Yet I woke up resenting these fine church people, but I was not sure why. And as I stumbled to the next city to meet with a group of pastors, I was still wondering.

During one session of the pastors conference, I asked each of the participants to write on a slip of paper their most pressing problem as a person in being a minister. Going through the slips, I was surprised to find that one of their main problems was resentment of the people in their churches. Some felt that the members used them in thoughtless ways which they would not think of using a business associate. Some thought their people had tried to extract every ounce of work they could out of their pastor for the smallest possible salary. There were many other problems, but they added up to a feeling that they were not being treated as persons but were used as religious equipment.

And then it hit me. I was as much a professional religionist as these pastors, and I was getting a small taste of that which many ministers live with constantly. People—many of whom love him dearly—thoughtlessly make extra demands and set up situations in which the minister either has to participate or appear to be selfish and un-Christian. The pastor in this trap often goes along, wanting to be God's servant. But because he is exhausted and the expectations are unreasonable, he begins to feel depressed—beyond mere physical exhaustion. And he feels a strange tightening in his stomach when additional meetings are called or added "duties" are dumped into his lap. What I had seen in my own experience was that these symptoms resulted from a repressed resentment of the very people I had flown a thousand miles to love for God's sake. It was terrible but true.

I saw that my problem as a professional was that I was still too concerned with my own feelings of happiness and satisfaction. I realized that I lacked a sort of divine disinterest in how I am treated. But on the other hand, I saw that we laymen are often "people eaters" in that we devour the personal life and creative love of our pastors and spokesmen by the way we use them and fail to help them. And the strange thing is that we never know what we are doing to them on the inside. Some of them resent us for it, but because they have been trained that such resentment indicates self-centeredness in a Christian, they must repress it. So, many ministers become discouraged, sick (physically or emotionally), or leave the ministry. And they feel guilty and bitter. (Of course many others are evidently emotionally wired for ceaseless activity and find their fulfillment in going constantly.)

But I now realize that my problem, as a layman, is that I have not been aware of the suffering of ministers—which means I have not loved them enough to be sensitive to their needs.

In my own case, as a traveling speaker, I had to make a
new beginning by confessing to God my resentment and frustration. I realized that a good bit of the problem that night
was *mine* for not establishing concrete limits and staying
roughly within them. This I can try to do in the future in
order to have an intelligent ministry when I travel. And I am
praying not to be so interested in *my* happiness and well-
being.

When I got home from that trip, I examined our attitudes
in our church and was appalled at what I saw. We seem to
expect our ministers to run the church with fewer staff people
than we would dream of allocating to an executive in a
business venture of comparable size. We say we love our
ministers and are very grateful for them. But somehow we do
not really look at their needs the way we do those of "normal
people."

It seems that I am so interested in my own hopes, dreams,
and projects that I use other people to the limit—and yet I
could not really recognize the extent of my own selfish tendency to use others . . . until it happened to me.

"Tell me how much you know of the sufferings of
your fellow men and I will tell you how much you have
loved them."[55]

Helmut Thielicke
*Our Heavenly Father*


"The longer I live, the more I feel that true repose
consists in 'renouncing' one's own self, by which I mean
making up one's mind to admit that there is no importance whatever in being 'happy' or 'unhappy' in the
usual meaning of the words. Personal success or personal satisfaction are not worth another thought if one
does achieve them, or worth worrying about if they

evade one or are slow in coming. All that is really worth while is action—faithful action, for the world, and in God. Before one can see that and live by it, there is a sort of threshold to cross, or a reversal to be made in what appears to be men's general habit of thought; but once that gesture has been made, what freedom is yours, freedom to work and to love! I have told you more than once that my life is now possessed by this 'disinterest' which I feel to be growing on me, while at the same time the deep-seated appetite, that calls me to all that is real at the heart of the real, continues to grow stronger."[56]

Pierre Teilhard de Chardin
*Letters from a Traveller*

LORD, forgive me. I was so intent on being treated well myself that I failed to see how thoughtless I often am in using the speakers I invite to visit our town. And I see in a hundred ways how I subtly use others to further my plans, and then send them on their way without realizing how they may feel. Thank You that it is not too late to look around and try to be more sensitive to the people with whom I work and live. Please give me the insight, the desire, and the strength to change.

FOR THE MINISTER IN ME:

"Do nothing from selfishness or conceit, but in humility count others better than yourselves. Let each of you look not only to his own interests, but also to the interests of others. Have this mind among yourselves, which you have in Christ Jesus, who, though he was in the form of God, did not count equality with God a thing to be grasped, but emptied himself, taking the form of a servant, being born in the likeness of men. And being found

in human form he humbled himself and became obedi-
ent unto death, even death on a cross. Therefore God has
highly exalted him and bestowed on him the name which
is above every name, that at the name of Jesus every
knee should bow, in heaven and on earth and under the
earth, and every tongue confess that Jesus Christ is
Lord, to the glory of God the Father."

Philippians 2:3–11

FOR THE LAYMAN IN ME:

"Bear one another's burdens, and so fulfill the law of
Christ. . . . Let him who is taught the word share all
good things with him who teaches. . . . So then, as we
have opportunity, let us do good to all men, and especially to those who are of the household of faith."

Galatians 6:2,6,10

# A View from Loner's Peak

YESTERDAY I talked to a very sharp and winsome man with a good sense of humor. Jack is a Christian minister, a district superintendent, whose position in his denomination makes him a pastor to fifty or sixty other ministers. He is handsome, intelligent, articulate, honest about himself, personally committed to Christ . . . and miserable.

As we talked, Jack told me that he felt basically lonely inside—even though he has a fine family and has done well in his vocation. He said that when he looked around at the other participants at ministers' meetings like the one we were attending, he felt as if many of his associates represented a kind of "in group" and had close personal friends with whom they came and roomed; but that he was not able to be as personal with other people as they seemed to be. In fact he felt that he had very few truly close personal friends at all, and that made him feel inadequate and lonely—even though he ministers to people constantly and is surrounded by "Christian friends."

As we talked, I thought about my own life inside and how often over the years I have felt like a "loner." I recall as a youngster moving to a new city and looking at groups of boys who seemed to be such close buddies and wishing I could be a real part of that which they seemed to be sharing. But then I

*166*

became a part of such groups, and later fraternities, and was a leader in several. I was surprised to learn that, except in rare instances, "in group" members are not nearly as loving and vulnerable to each other about their real problems and aspirations as they appeared to be *from the outside*. I discovered the "façade of intimacy" which in-groups often wear. Some groups are together so much because their individual members' identity is wrapped up in their association with the group, rather than because of any deep personal relationships with its members. But this façade of intimacy is a well-guarded secret, a secret which makes probably millions of kids and adults feel inadequate if they do not have "lots of close friends who are 'in.' "

I am an outgoing person and have always moved toward people. Yet inwardly I am shy and reticent about imposing myself on those with whom I would most like to be friends. But as I have counseled with men and women who are successful materially and socially these past few years, I have found myself identifying with their feelings of inadequacy in this area of life so often that I began asking some of them how many really close personal friends they had. Many replied, "None." Some said, "One or two," but almost no one had more than five or six. After having moved more than a dozen times in twenty years of marriage, I realize that although there are many people we love, respond to, and enjoy being with on occasion, there are only a handful of people we feel are close friends.

All this made me wonder if perhaps many of us have been subtly conditioned to look for something which actually does not exist, except in a few cases—a place in life with a large number of intimate, totally open friends. In a busy active life one has the time and energy to be real friends with only a very few people on a continuing basis.

The lonely district superintendent with whom I was talking

yesterday seemed to be feeling guilty, rejected, and inadequate because he could not get a group of other district
superintendents to be totally open and loving friends. But as I
talked to some of the other men at the conference, I found that
most of them were guarded about being open concerning their
personal lives to anyone. Because of vocational vulnerability,
it may be even more difficult for ministers to be part of an
open sharing group, where each member reveals his true needs
and inadequacies, than it is for laymen. But the desire seems
to be intense to satisfy this restless longing to find like-minded
people with whom one can share the trials and joys of life. A
person who feels that he is in a subordinate role will not do
for this kind of friendship. So it would seem that ministers
are fortunate to have one close friend with whom they can be
totally honest.

I believe this restless yearning for completeness in relationships is universal. And although we try to fulfill it
through friends, mates, and children, it seems to me that this
restlessness can never truly be satisfied by people. I am becoming convinced that this deepest unrest is a longing for
complete union with God, which is planted in the fabric of
every man's life. Maybe Augustine was right when he said
that our hearts will always be restless until we find our ultimate rest in Him.

In my own life, I am more relaxed about my peers than I
ever have been. I feel closer to people with whom I work and
pray, since I do not expect them to fulfill an interprersonal
need which can be met only by God. And paradoxically, some
of us are becoming to each other the deeply sharing friends
for whom I have always longed.

••◄◆►••

"Great priests, saints like the Curé d'Ars, who have
seen into the hidden depths of thousands of souls, have,
nevertheless, remained men with few intimate friends.

No one is more lonely than a priest who has a vast ministry. He is isolated in a terrible desert by the secrets of his fellow men."[57]

Thomas Merton
*No Man Is an Island*

" 'A friend is one soul in two bodies.' Yet friendship implies few friends rather than many; he who has many friends has no 'friend'; and 'to be a friend to many people in the way of perfect friendship is impossible.' Fine friendship requires duration rather than fitful intensity . . ."[58]

Aristotle, *Ethics*

··+·◆◄▮▸◆·+··

LORD, give me the grace not to try to force other people to give me the kind of unconditional acceptance and love that only You have to give. Help me not to reject them when they cannot be You. Thank You that in Christ *You* have offered to be the personal friend I have longed for—in whose unconditional love and acceptance I can sometimes find the courage to reach out to others. Help me to risk their rejection in order to introduce them to You and Your truth about living as a son in this complex world. Although I hate to admit it, I am glad that You went through the experience in Christ and with Paul of having to go it alone without friends during some trying times. It is comforting to know that you understand the feelings of a loner.

··+·◆◄▮▸◆·+··

JESUS:
. . . "Then all the disciples forsook him and fled."
Matthew 26:56

"And about the ninth hour Jesus cried with a loud voice . . . 'My God, my God, why hast thou forsaken me?' "
Matthew 27:46

AND PAUL:

"Do your best to come to me soon. For Demas, in love
with this present world, has deserted me and gone to
Thessalonica; Crescens has gone to Galatia, Titus to
Dalmatia. Luke alone is with me . . . At my first defense no one took my part; all deserted me . . ."

II Timothy 4:9–11, 16

# Confessions of a False Prophet

FOR A LONG time after I became a Christian I did not
speak about my faith publicly. But several years ago I
began to travel and talk about the Christian life as it was
unfolding in my own experience as a business man.

This was a good experience but a strange thing began to
happen. As I traveled further and further from home, wrote a
book, and spoke to larger groups, some people quit reacting
to me as an ordinary layman who had made an exciting
personal discovery. Certain individuals began to react to me
as something other than a struggling Christian. A few started
to treat me as some sort of "authority" or a "program personality" and to look after my physical comfort with great care
and thoughtfulness when I was with them. I found this very
pleasant. As a matter of fact, without ever realizing it, I
began to expect this little bit of special care and status which
was more and more being accorded me. And, although I have
only seen it in retrospect, I noticed occasionally more than a
tinge of resentment for those people who invited me to speak
and did *not* make adequate arrangements for me while I was
in their city. After all, I thought, I was often exhausted, since
traveling and being with people constantly is very tiring for
me.

But then it occurred to me what was happening. I was becoming the thing I have rebelled against all my life: a pampered professional religionist. With a kind of shocked thoughtfulness I could see what sometimes happens to ministers, bishops, and traveling evangelists. People seal them into a sort of emotionally padded traveling litter and pass them from one religious group or situation to another. They do not treat such visiting pros the same way they treat other men at all. The difference is very subtle and built into our social response system; and most people do not seem to realize that they are treating "religious speakers" with such deference.

But after a while the effect can be very corroding to the speaker's integrity. At one level or another he begins in self-defense to fit the role expected of him and become a religious authority, instead of a person who wants to live out his life trying to find and do God's will. And if a speaker surrenders to this temptation to be "outstanding," there is a fantastic danger, it appears to me, of becoming an "approval-holic": hooked on constant favorable attention and approval instead of alcohol. When I move in this direction it affects subtly but deeply the *content* of my speaking as well as its freshness. I unconsciously tone down the unpleasant aspects of that which I am saying and accentuate those things which affirm the group's existing beliefs and prejudices. And before long I will have justified the whole procedure by telling myself that I should be gentle and go slowly with people.

Several ministers over the years have told me in one way or another, "Keith, I really believe in a committed life. But my people are not ready for that kind of commitment yet, or that kind of confrontation." So they admit they preach something less than the best they know and have experienced, because they are afraid people "are not ready" for the best. But when this happened to me recently and I said these same words to myself, I discovered that I meant by them that it was *I* who was not ready to risk a certain group's rejection of *me* if I said things which were too threatening to their beliefs . . . and thus to the status quo. So for that night I became what the Scriptures call a "false prophet," more interested in material approval than in speaking any creative, freeing truth God had given me.

But the tragedy is that with all of my recognition of and rebellion against these things, I find myself very subtly doing them. At the time my reasons seem so sound, and sometimes I realize they are sound. And often I catch myself and do speak the truth as I see it. But here in this time of prayer I know that I am still so often full of myself and concerned about what people think of me. And I know that I am deeply a part of the problem for which Christ died.

·+·❧❦☙·+·

A PROPHET:

"He broke fresh ground—because, and only because, he had the courage to go ahead without asking whether others were following or even understood. He had no need for the divided responsibility in which others seek to be safe from ridicule, because he had been granted a faith which required no confirmation—a contact with reality, light and intense like the touch of a loved hand; a union in self-surrender without self-destruction, where his heart was lucid and his mind loving . . ."

CHARACTER OR TOLERANCE?

"All too easily we confuse a fear of standing up for our beliefs, a tendency to be more influenced by the convictions of others than by our own, or simply a lack of conviction—with the need that the strong and mature feel to give full weight to the arguments of the other side. A game of hide-and-seek: when the devil wishes to play on our lack of character, he calls it tolerance, and when he wants to stifle our first attempts to learn tolerance, he calls it lack of character."[59]

Dag Hammarskjold
*Markings*

⋅⋅◆❈◆⋅⋅

LORD, help me to begin again with Your strength and Spirit, and to be one of the free children of Your family. Help me to speak to please You and not important or brilliant people. Allow me to transmit something of the love and creative courage You showed us in Christ. Forgive me when I am afraid to chance rejection or failure. But thank You for the times I am willing to risk being vulnerable in love. May their number increase.

⋅⋅◆❈◆⋅⋅

". . . though we had already suffered and been shamefully treated at Philippi, as you know, we had courage in our God to declare to you the gospel of God in the face of great opposition. For our appeal does not spring from error or uncleanness, nor is it made with guile; but just as we have been approved by God to be entrusted with the gospel, so we speak, not to please men, but to please God who tests our hearts."

I Thessalonians 2:2–4

# The Gamble of Faith

YESTERDAY MORNING I woke up restless and vaguely afraid . . . of what I wasn't sure. Then I remembered: in the mail the day before I had received a letter from a dear friend. He had just been advised by his doctor that he had between two weeks and three months to live because of a malignancy which had reached his liver. I was deeply shaken and grieved. The vague anxieties I had felt earlier blossomed into concrete fears, and I began to imagine all kinds of bad things happening.

Over a year ago I decided to devote my time to writing professionally, without the support of a regular job. But I have been doing so much public speaking and traveling that I worry about not getting any writing done and not being able to make a living for my family. As the specters danced out of the shadowy corners into my conscious mind, I imagined Mary Allen's death and my great loneliness at her dying . . . the children had grown up and left home . . . I was a lonely old man. Then, like a jack-in-the-box, out jumped the specter of my own death, and I was afraid. I did not know in that instant whether I believed in Christ or even in God the Father. I experienced the great emptiness of death, was horrified . . . and desperately wanted proof and certainty.

*175*

But as I saw these things and faced the panic they brought, I also grasped again with pristine clarity the deep human meaning of the gospel of Jesus Christ for me. "Let not your hearts be troubled . . ." (Jn. 14:1), "I go to prepare a place for you . . ." (Jn. 14:3), "be of good cheer, I have overcome the world" (Jn. 16:33). I saw that I could not capture faith once and for all time and put it in a box for safekeeping. In the face of death and possible failure in my own life or in the lives of those I love, I could not even *know* for sure that "God is."

"What am I going to do?" I thought, trying not to give in to the wave of desperation I felt was about to break over me. I had lived with faith for years, and it seemed to be crumbling all around me. Then I knew. All I could do, to come to terms with my own death, was to bet my life that Jesus Christ "is for real," and give Him my whole future.

It became evident to me again that this Christian Way is not often entered through the lofty door of philosophical reasoning, but through a wager, a bet with fantastic stakes.* Because of those things I have seen and heard in my own experience and in the lives of many others across the years, I have bet my life that God *is,* and that He is the kind of love which walked around in the life and actions of Jesus Christ. I have wagered that He even loves me and wants me to be related as a child to Him. And when out of great need, I have made this bet, I have stepped into a new dimension of life— life in which there is hope in history because God is at the end of the road for me and for all of us.

---

* This notion of a wager may seem strange or not respectable. I got the idea from Blaise Pascal the 17th-century mathematical genius who had a profound Christian conversion. As he pointed out, one makes the wager that God is or is not either consciously or implicitly by his behavior. I am just suggesting that it has been helpful to me to make it explicit. See Pascal's *Pensées.*

Now, although I still cannot *know* that God is real, I somehow *do* know. Even though I cannot prove it to you or even make the bet for you, I can say this: for me, these seem to be the only two alternatives—to live a phony life of frantic hiding from myself and of psychological repression of thoughts about death and meaning. Or to face death and life and make this strange gamble of faith which turns me outward toward other people and makes me want to be a loving person. I can see no other way for me than following Christ.

··+‹‹§|§›+··

"We all want to be certain, we all want proof, but the kind of proof that we tend to want—scientifically or philosophically demonstrable proof that would silence all doubts once and for all—would not in the long run, I think answer the fearful depths of our need at all. For what we need to know, of course, is not just that God exists, not just that beyond the steely brightness of the stars there is a cosmic intelligence of some kind that keeps the whole show going, but that there is a God right here in the thick of our day-by-day lives who may not be writing messages about Himself in the stars but who in one way or another is trying to get messages through our blindness as we move around down here knee-deep in the fragrant muck and misery and marvel of the world. It is not objective proof of God's existence that we want but, whether we use religious language for it or not, the experience of God's presence. That is the miracle that we are really after. And that is also, I think, the miracle that we really get."[60]

Frederick Buechner
*The Magnificent Defeat*

··+‹‹§|§›+··

LORD, I do love You. And I am very grateful that this relationship with You has been so often one of hope and a sense of expansion into a larger and more interesting journey. But occasionally there are these times of dread and doubt which bring me to my knees in awe. I see again that faith is a gift of grace, and that all the figuring and reasoning in the world cannot transpose me across the void between us and You. Thank You that in Christ You have provided the leap of faith, the fantastic wager of life.

"I sought the Lord, and he answered me, and delivered me from all my fears."

Psalm 34:4

# Renewal in the Church—But Who Cares Enough?

B UT THE PEOPLE don't really care that much," the bright, young minister was saying in a thoughtful but discouraged tone. We had just finished a series of meetings in his church, and he had gotten a large group of apparently interested men and women out for every session. I had just said that it was obvious he had done some work among these people—especially since so many ministers had told me that they could not motivate their congregations to do anything besides attend Sunday services.

But this very perceptive young man saw beyond the meetings into the people's lives. He knew that his affluent congregation was really living for money, social status, and power. And he saw that all this "church business" was only a small part of a more important social life for most of his members. "How can people like this ever be vehicles for new life in the Church?" he asked, shaking his head in answer to his own question. He smiled philosophically as he shook my hand at gate No. 4, and I got on the plane for New York and Boston.

I tried to settle down in a coach window seat, hoping to relax a few minutes before the next churchful of strangers.

*179*

Thinking about the congregation I had just left and its young pastor's remarks, I began to feel that he was right: people whose imaginations are captured by the world—even the good things in it including church business—are not going to be motivated strongly enough to take the risks and discipline necessary for genuine newness to come in the Church. But what kind of people will be motivated to stick with it?

I did not want to think about it any more, so I closed my eyes and prayed: "God, I'm tired—tired of thinking about these same problems, tired of traveling, tired of being a misfit in a generation going in a different direction from the one I've chosen." As I continued talking to God, I found myself saying, "But I wouldn't trade what I've found in this relationship with You for all the geographical settledness in the world. I guess I just remember too well the fear and blankness of living without You. Somehow Your presence and acceptance here and now make this perpetual wandering seem almost like a home."

Opening my eyes, I smiled at the hostess, accepting a cup of coffee. I had been in a semi-conscious state, pretty oblivious of the plane. But I waked up with a deep conviction about new life in the institutional church: I was convinced that "Christian renewal" will be accomplished—where it takes place with any lasting depth—through the lives of a group of desperate people who are personally finding irreplaceable hope and meaning in living for Christ and His purposes among men. Because, as the young minister had said so perceptively, the ordinary busy churchmen "really don't care that much."

·+‹⊹⊱⊰⊹›+·

[Christian meets Worldly Wisdom who tries to dissuade him from going on the Christian pilgrimage] "I am older than thou; thou art like to meet with, in the way which thou goest, wearisomeness, painfulness, hunger, perils, nakedness, sword, lions, dragons, darkness, and, in a word, death, and what not . . . And why should a man so carelessly cast away himself by giving heed to a stranger [and going on]?

"Christian: Why, sir, this burden upon my back is more terrible to me than are all these things which you have mentioned: nay, me thinks I care not what I meet with in the way, if so be I can also meet with deliverance from my burden."[61]

John Bunyan
*Pilgrim's Progress*

"For the son of God did not come from above to add an external form of worship to the several ways of life that are in the world, and so leave people to live as they did before. But he came down from heaven altogether divine and heavenly in his own nature to call mankind to a divine and heavenly life; to the highest change of their own nature; to be born again of the Holy Spirit; to walk in the wisdom and light of God; to be like him to the utmost of their power; to renounce all the most plausible ways of the world; and to live in such wisdom, purity, and holiness as might fit them to be glorious in the enjoyment of God to all eternity."[62]

William Law
*A Serious Call to a Devout and
Holy Life*

LORD, thank You that we are only asked to penetrate the world and not engulf it. I am grateful You intimated that a little salt—a few committed people—can do the job of changing the taste of the whole banquet of life to which You have invited all men. Help me to seek out those other men and women in Your Church whose needs are such that they cannot live without You, those other people who clearly know they need a Physician. Bring us to life, Lord, as Your people. Help us to wake up; and fill us with the power and the Spirit to be Your gentle giants in the world, in which we live as Your hesitant children.

··+‹‹‹¦¦¦›+··

"Besides this you know what hour it is, how it is full time now for you to wake from sleep. For salvation is nearer to us now than when we first believed; the night is far gone, the day is at hand. Let us then cast off the works of darkness and put on the armor of light."

Romans 13:11,12

# I Needed My Past

SOMETIMES WHEN ONE of our children feels rejected by a group, or thinks she is unattractive and unacceptable, my stomach tightens and I ache for them. I want to run and hold my little girl and protect her from the pain and rejection of the world. But at such moments I am never sure exactly how to pray. Because every time the situation comes up, I remember Alice's face one night many years ago.

We were in a small group of adults who were struggling together to learn how to pray and to live as Christians. We were getting acquainted by going around the room, each telling the others some things about his childhood. One older lady had had a good many disappointments and seemed bitter about her past. Then it was Alice's turn. She spoke to us hesitantly.

"When I was a tiny little girl, I was put in an orphanage. I was not pretty at all, and no one wanted me. But I can recall longing to be adopted and loved by a family as far back as I can remember. I thought about it day and night. But everything I did seemed to go wrong. I tried too hard to please everybody who came to look me over, and all I did was drive people away. Then one day the head of the orphanage told me a family was going to come and take me home with them. I was so excited, I jumped up and down and cried. The matron reminded me that I was on trial and that it might not be a permanent arrangement. But I just knew it would be. So I went with this family and started to school in their town—a very happy little girl. And life began to open for me, just a little.

"But one day, a few months later, I skipped home from school and ran in the front door of the big old house we lived in. No one was at home, but there in the middle of the front hall was my battered old suitcase with my little coat thrown over it. As I stood there and looked at that suitcase, it slowly dawned on me what it meant . . . they didn't want me. And I hadn't even suspected."

Alice stopped speaking a moment, but we didn't notice. We were each standing in that front hall with the high ceiling, looking at the battered suitcase and trying not to cry. Then Alice cleared her throat and said almost matter-of-factly, "That happened to me seven times before I was thirteen years old."

I looked at this tall, forty-year-old, gray-haired woman sitting across the room and wept. I had just met Alice, but I found myself loving her and feeling a great compassion for her. She looked up, surprised and touched at what had happened to us as we had responded to her story. But she held up her hand and shook her head slightly, in a gesture to stop us from feeling sorry for her. "Don't," she said with a genuinely happy smile, "I *needed* my past. You see—it brought me to God."

⁕⋙⋘⁕

"Can this be true? Is there any greater wretchedness than to taste the dregs of our own insufficiency and misery and hopelessness, and to know that we are certainly worth nothing at all? Yet it is blessed to be reduced to these depths if, in them, we can find God. Until we have reached the bottom of the abyss, there is still something for us to choose between all and nothing. There is still something in between. We can still evade the decision. When we are reduced to our last extreme, there is no further evasion. The choice is a terrible one. It is made in the heart of darkness, but with an intuition that is unbearable by its angelic clarity: when we who have been destroyed and seem to be in hell miraculously choose God!"[63]

Thomas Merton
*No Man Is an Island*

DEAR LORD, help me to remember that You did not promise to take us out of the problems of the world, but that You did promise to be with us as we face them. Give me the faith and the courage to let my children live and take their knocks without panicking. And when they fail, help me to stand by them as they try to pick up the pieces and move into the future. Help me to give them support but not to over-protect them from the difficulties of growing up, since I remember that I, like Alice, needed the problems of my past to bring me to You.

"Indeed I count everything as loss because of the surpassing worth of knowing Christ Jesus my Lord. For his sake I have suffered the loss of all things, and count them as refuse, in order that I may gain Christ and be found in him, not having a righteousness of my own, based on law, but that which is through faith in Christ, the righteousness from God that depends on faith; that I may know him and the power of his resurrection, and may share his sufferings, becoming like him in his death, that if possible I may attain the resurrection from the dead."

Philippians 3:8–11

# Notes

1. Dietrich Bonhoeffer, *Prisoner for God* (New York: The Macmillan Company, 1961), p. 52.

2. Louis Fischer, *Gandhi, His Life and Message for the World* (New York: Mentor Books, 1960), p. 33f.

3. Viktor E. Frankl, *Man's Search for Meaning* (New York: Washington Square Press, Inc., 1964), p. 158.

4. William James, *The Varieties of Religious Experience* (New York: The Modern Library, 1929), pp. 452, 453.

5. Martin Luther, *Luther's Works* (Philadelphia: Muhlenburg Press, 1959), Vol. 36, p. 86.

6. Paul Tournier, *The Meaning of Persons* (New York: Harper and Row, Publishers, 1957), pp. 36, 37.

7. J. S. Whale, *Christian Doctrine* (Cambridge: The University Press, 1956), pp. 145, 146.

8. C. G. Jung, *The Collected Works* (New York: Pantheon Press, 1960), Vol. 8, see pp. 45–61.

9. Martin Luther, *Luther's Works* (St. Louis: Concordia Publishing House, 1959), Vol. 23, p. 73.

10. Thomas à Kempis, *The Imitation of Christ* (London: Collins, 1957), p. 90.

11. Paul Tournier, *Guilt and Grace* (New York: Harper and Row, Publishers, 1962), pp. 85, 86.

12. Paul Tournier, *The Adventure of Living* (New York: Harper and Row, Publishers, 1963), p. 116.

13. Fr. William McNamara, *The Art of Being Human* (Milwaukee: The Bruce Publishing Company, 1962), p. 69.

14. Rollo May, *The Art of Counseling* (New York: Abingdon-Cokesbury Press, 1939).

15. Will Durant, *The Story of Philosophy* (New York: Garden City Publishing Company, Inc., 1943), p. 52.

16. Alfred Adler, *Psychologies of 1930*, ed. Carl Murchison (Worcester, Mass.: Clark University Press, 1930), see chapter 21, "Individual Psychology."

17. William Temple, *Nature, Man and God* (New York: The Macmillan Company, 1956), p. 233.

18. Augustine, Bishop of Hippo, *The Confessions of St. Augustine* (New York: E. P. Dutton and Company, Inc., 1951), p. 187.

19. Lorenzo Scupoli, *Unseen Warfare* (London: Faber and Faber Limited, 1952), pp. 31, 32.

20. Paul Tillich, *The Shaking of the Foundations* (London: SCM Press, 1949).

21. Whale, *op. cit.*

22. Thomas Merton, *No Man Is an Island* (New York: Harcourt, Brace and World, Inc., 1955), p. 5.

23. Father Andrew, *The Life and Letters of Father Andrew*, ed. Kathleen E. Burne (London: A. R. Mowbray and Co., 1961), p. 166.

24. John Knox, *Life in Jesus Christ* (New York: Seabury Press, 1966), pp. 125, 126.

25. William Temple, *Readings in St. John's Gospel* (London: The Macmillan Company, Ltd., 1963), p. 24.

26. Sigmund Freud, *A General Introduction to Psychoanalysis* (New York: Washington Square Press, Inc.), p. 22.

27. William Barclay, *Turning to God* (London: Epworth Press, 1963), pp. 40, 41.

28. Frederick Buechner, *The Magnificent Defeat* (New York: The Seabury Press, 1966), p. 47.

29. D. Elton Trueblood, *A Place to Stand* (New York: Harper and Row, Publishers, 1969), p. 43.

30. Scupoli, *op. cit.*, pp. 96, 97.

31. Fischer, *op. cit.*, p. 33.

32. Scupoli, *op. cit.*

33. Thomas à Kempis, *op. cit.*, pp. 148, 149.

34. Frederick B. Speakman, *The Salty Tang* (Westwood, New Jersey: Fleming H. Revell Company, 1954), p. 97.

35. Paul Tournier, *The Meaning of Persons* (New York: Harper and Row, Publishers, 1957), p. 22.

36. Scupoli, *op. cit.*, p. 175.

37. Martin Buber, *I and Thou* (New York: Charles Scribner's Sons, 1958), p. 127.

38. Aurelius Augustinus, *The City of God* (New York: Modern Library, 1950), Book xxi, chapter vii, p. 776.

39. Blaise Pascal, *Pascal's Pensées* (New York: E. P. Dutton and Co., Inc., 1958).

40. Alfred North Whitehead, *Adventure of Ideas* (New York: Mentor Books, 1960), p. 160.

41. Buechner, *op. cit.*, p. 23.

42. Reuel Howe, *The Miracle of Dialogue* (Greenwich, Conn.: The Seabury Press, 1963), p. 93.

43. Dag Hammarskjold, *Markings* (New York: Alfred A. Knopf, 1966), p. 133.

44. Temple, *op. cit.*, p. 243.

45. Bonhoeffer, *op. cit.*, pp. 141, 142.

46. C. W. Morris, *Signs, Language and Behavior* (New York: Prentice Hall, 1946).

47. Morris E. Eson, *Psychological Foundations of Education* (New York: Holt, Rinehart and Winston, Inc., 1965), p. 39.

48. Howe, *op. cit.*, p. 124.

49. James, *op. cit.*, p. 243.

50. Thomas à Kempis, *op. cit.*, p. 181.

51. John Donne, *Private Devotions* (Ann Arbor, Michigan: The University of Michigan Press, 1959), p. 27.

52. Nels F. S. Ferré, *Faith and Reason* (New York: Harper and Row, Publishers, 1946), pp. 234, 235, footnote.

53. C. S. Lewis, "The Episcopalian," February 1964, p. 23.

54. James, *op. cit.*, p. 456.

55. Helmut Thielicke, *Our Heavenly Father* (New York: Harper and Row, Publishers, 1960), p. 93.

56. Pierre Teilhard De Chardin, *Letters from a Traveller* (New York: Harper and Row, Publishers, 1962), p. 160.

57. Merton, *op. cit.*, p. 12.

58. Durant, *op. cit.*, p. 62.

59. Hammarskjold, *op. cit.*, p. 110.

60. Buechner, *op. cit.*

61. John Bunyan, *Pilgrim's Progress* (New York: The Mershon Company), p. 14, 15.

62. William Law, *A Serious Call to a Devout and Holy Life* (Philadelphia: The Westminster Press, 1955), p. 69.

63. Merton, *op. cit.*, p. 208.